Work Online: Become a Solopreneur, Start Working Remotely. The Complete Guide to Grow Your Company on the Internet.

Daniel D. Coffman

Published by Creafe Publishing, 2023.

While every precaution has been taken in the preparation of this book, the publisher assumes no responsibility for errors or omissions, or for damages resulting from the use of the information contained herein.

WORK ONLINE: BECOME A SOLOPRENEUR, START WORKING REMOTELY. THE COMPLETE GUIDE TO GROW YOUR COMPANY ON THE INTERNET.

First edition. September 15, 2023.

ISBN: 979-8223448198

Written by Daniel D. Coffman.

Also by Daniel D. Coffman

Freelance Consulting: Provide Services to High Ticket Customers. Build and Grow Your own Gig Empire.

Work Online: Become a Solopreneur, Start Working Remotely. The Complete Guide to Grow Your Company on the Internet.

Table of Contents

Introduction..1

Chapter one | How to become a solopreneur and lead an independent life ... 17

Chapter two | Start working remotely.. 31

Chapter three | 12 things you didn't intend for as you launched hiring remote workers 57

Chapter three | The complete guide to grow your company on the web. 71

Chapter four | 15 important actions to starting and growing your own online business 93

Chapter five | Online working 105

Introduction

The expression "solopreneur", although not brand new, has gained recognition recently as a means to describe the expanding amount of "solo entrepreneurs" on the market now. And although there's a good deal of overlap between an entrepreneur and a solopreneur, there are subtle distinctions to be made between them both.

In this guide, you will learn about the differences between a solopreneur along with also an entrepreneur. You'll also find out how to develop into a prosperous solopreneur and flourish.

The differences

Solopreneurs put a high value. By definition, a solopreneur is really a 1 person operation.

By comparison, an entrepreneur is currently building a group of folks who focus on specific regions of the company. Think earnings, bookkeeping, customer support etc..

A solopreneur, on the flip side, is accountable for each and every element of the business enterprise. That does not signify they don't need assistance, but more about this later.

Since solopreneurs by character work independently, most often to be introverts. Should you require a group dynamic so as to get your creative juices flowing to remain effective, solopreneurship may not be to you.

And since solopreneurs do not have workers that work given hours they could normally set their own program. This may be a double edged sword. It supplies exactly the solopreneur the flexibility to take some time off as required, but without ego motivation, the company will not survive.

The similarities

The two solopreneurs and entrepreneurs build real companies. Sometimes folks think about this solopreneur as somebody with a profitable avocation or somebody that has "established a project to themselves". And while this might be true for a few, the great majority of solopreneurs are creating real companies that offer a constant stream of recurring income which builds wealth.

The two strive to create companies which could be sustained by themselves and need minimal supervision to keep. The two solopreneurs and entrepreneurs are developing companies which could be sustainable with minimum supervision. The entrepreneur does so by placing a management group in place so the provider runs economically in their lack. The solopreneur utilizes methods of automation to attain exactly the exact same outcome.

All successful companies must begin with a creator that has a crystal clear vision of what it is that they would like to achieve. Thus both solopreneurs and entrepreneurs establish long term objectives and short-term goals which are clearly defined and quantifiable to be able to monitor their achievement.

The two will also be self-determined. Self determination is that the notion your payoff (or earnings) is directly proportional to the effort that you put in. To put it differently, as a worker, should you create a sale which produces $1,000,000 for your business, you merely receive a small number of the as a commission. However, as a solopreneur you have the whole quantity.

The advantages of solopreneurship

There are a variety reasons which people turn into solopreneurs. The urge to become your own boss, dissatisfaction with present job, flexible work schedule, much more family/vacation period plus obviously a higher income possible. However, there are some additional, maybe not so apparent advantages to becoming a solopreneur offering:

Expand your ability sets

Since you're liable for all elements of your business enterprise, it compels you to handle all of the issues which will inevitably arise in each area.

Perhaps not so great at keeping up a site? Do not stress, it will gradually return forcing you to work out how to repair it.

Perhaps not proficient in the sales or people speaking? You'll be when your income is dependent upon it.

However, do not worry, even after a time, all solopreneurs become used to those things and quite soon you are going to be carrying them since they come.

Can function on the main sections of your small business

As a worker, you're made to endure a great deal of things which are entirely (un) or perhaps counterproductive to the mission of the business. Consider just how many useless meetings you have had to sit through, or just how many reports you've needed to create or paperwork you needed to fill out this has been completely ineffective. That's a great deal of non productive actions which you must execute.

As a solopreneur, you're freed from all of the frivolous cya paperwork and you may focus on the most effective components of your company.

Could "switch on a dime"

In today's fast paced world, having the capability to adapt to changing marketplace requirements is the secret to developing a prosperous business enterprise. As a solopreneur, you've got the best versatility in this field. With no shareholders, investors, board members or perhaps personnel, you can correct your plans and execute them quite quickly.

Kinds of firms which are best for that the solopreneur

Obviously not all sorts of companies are appropriate to a solopreneur. If you would like to really produce a product, then you still will need to get a tangible construction with employees and machines so as to create this item. However there are a great deal of web based companies that are fantastic for the solopreneur.

Virtual assistant

A digital assistant is a person who assists others with (largely) mundane tasks such as resizing and answering email, scheduling appointments and societal websites direction. All of these are actions which take a large quantity of time and people will happily pay other people to do.

Blogger

This is among the most well-known ways individuals become solopreneurs. Begin by selecting a topic (or market) which you presently are interested in and begin creating content about this topic. After that, participate in groups which share a similar fascination and donate.

This combination of producing quality articles and media with other people will increase the audience for the site. As soon as you create an audience, you are able to monetize it by advertising advertisements and or affiliate advertising.

Ebook writer

If writing is the thing, getting an ebook author might be right up your street. Most of us know how challenging it is to get a first-time author to become published. Lucky for one of the world wide web has made it possible for nearly everyone to become published.

By writing publications in digital form, you will not have any printing expenses. And seeing as you're selling the publication, you must keep 100 percent of their profits. And yes, you may also market your book on amazon (even though they may take a proportion of their sales cost).

Graphic designer

If the visual arts will be more your thing, getting a freelancer graphic designer might be to you personally. Graphic designers help businesses designing logos and other visual articles to help boost a firm's identity and logo new.

Life coach

Why are you a people person? Then turning into a life coach is a thing to take into account. You may work with people helping them with things such as finance and budgeting, business and maybe even household and individual relationships. This can be achieved using skype, email or perhaps over the telephone.

We have simply gone above a very few of those companies which are appropriate to your solopreneur. There are a whole lot more you can select from. Matters like podcaster, event planner, mentor, handyman, traveling advisor and a lot more. Your chances are nearly infinite.

How to succeed as a solopreneur

Getting a solopreneur could be enjoyable, rewarding and rewarding. Nonetheless, it's also a great deal of work. From time to time, people become overwhelmed at the notion of doing themselves. So below are a few hints you may use to lower the weight and become a thriving solopreneur.

1. Have a good plan

Just like every company, it is vital that you establish goals both short and long term so you can measure your own progress. To this end, you need to create a mission statement and a vision statement which you are able to refer down to the street.

Your plan should comprise four elements

· how are you going to develop your company?

· are you planning for this growth?

· how can you intend to make passive income?

· are you going to be expanding by incorporating extra services or products?

If you're able to map from where you would like to be, you will have a far easier time.

2. You do not have to move it

One among the most intimidating things of becoming a solopreneur is the sum of work demanded. After all, even in case you are responsible for sales, advertising, customer support, bookkeeping, advertizing, branding, sociable websites and much more, it becomes overwhelming.

However, here is the fantastic news, you do not need to go it alone. There are tons of different solopreneurs out there inclined to have the tasks which you cannot or simply don't wish to perform. These people today specialize in services such as web site development, email advertising, copywriting, bookkeeping, graphic design, sociable networking direction, and far more. By employing these additional solopreneurs, it is going to free up you focus on the most effective regions of your company.

Recall at the beginning once I explained that, simply because a solopreneur does not have workers, it does not signify they don't need help? This is precisely what I mean. It's possible to receive all the advantages of a worker without each the frustrations by using salespeople and paying for the job you require.

3. Do not be scared into "pivot"

All too often we receive a vision within our thoughts of how things will need to proceed or what they ought to be like. However, the world does not actually work like that. Circumstances change, markets change and also client's flavor's change.

Be willing to correct your priorities, aims and also your own vision of this enterprise to coincide with those modifications. In the end, this is 1 place in which you, as a solopreneur have a massive edge over your bigger competitors.

4. Do not be in contest with anybody but yourself

Attempting to compare yourself to other people is obviously a losing match.

First importantly, you will forever supporting somebody, and before others. We have a tendency to always concentrate on who is facing us, rather than who is behind us. This is an error on 2 counts. By just focusing on who's facing us, we might overlook that individual behind us who develop a new approach and is going to leave everybody in the dust.

Second and more to the point, it is too easy to become frustrated and give up if you're continuously watching your progress rather than measuring up to other people. Plus, do not forget that you're simply comparing to others would like you to view. Most of us put our very best foot forward in people scenarios however, nobody actually understands what it is like for different men and women.

In brief, the very best way to advance is to celebrate all of your successes, both big and small and remain inspired.

5. Automation

This is your very best buddy of this solopreneur. You need to always attempt to automate as much of this job as you can.

Use email autoresponders to promote to clients. Use revenue funnels to obtain clients and promote goods. Use social networking monitoring applications to produce normal posts.

There is a great deal of automation applications available now, make the most of it!

15 personal aims for work that will assist you succeed

It is simple to blend in the crowd on the job. Nearly all employees decide to settle for mediocrity and anonymity; particularly if they operate at a big or digital work atmosphere. It is a whole lot easier to go to work daily and contribute only enough to satisfy your job's needs than it would be to make an enduring impression in your colleagues.

What is not simple is standing outside.

By setting personal targets for work, you're able to deliberately work towards becoming detected that can propel you in obtaining your dream project.

Do not settle for mediocrity and don't pay for anonymity. Dream big and stick out in the audience. Listed below are 15 examples of private aims for work that will assist you stick out from the colleagues and direct a thriving career.

1. Self-mastery

Self-mastery is about broadening your knowledge of your abilities, strengths and flaws. When you recognize what makes you special and what you are most passionate about, use that consciousness to develop your abilities even further.

Use your comprehension of your flaws to spot areas of development. By devoting yourself-awareness in these regions, you may demonstrate the opportunity to self control your growth and expansion.

2. Being grateful for where you're

Require a minute and reflect upon just how hard you've had to get where you are now.

How many occasions did you apply to your project? How many interviews did you go through? How many hours have you set up?

You have worked hard to reach where you are now. Be thankful of each the hard work you have put into get you wherever you are now.

By practising gratitude, you open up yourself to get what is next.

3. Staying excited for what is next

The perfect vibrational position to be into become actively working towards your own aims will be always to exercise gratitude for your existing situation and also to feel enthusiasm for what is coming.

Anticipate better things to come. Expect you will reach your target and that you are working towards your dream project. Be open to getting what is coming your way.

4. Celebrating every others' differences

As colleagues, most of us bring different strengths into a group atmosphere. Introverts bring profound notion to present issues and extroverts succeed in meetings and talks. The myers-briggs form indicator is an superb dimension of character differences and provides an intriguing review of your group's characters interact with one another.

If possible, ask to get an mbti performed along with your colleagues so you are able to find out more about your similarities and gaps; or comprehend the gaps on your group's characters and value they each contribute various values to this category.

5. Utilizing your team's differences for your edge

After you find out more about different personalities on your group, you can perform more smartly with your colleagues. Some colleagues may pose as introverts who would rather take away time to review advice prior to making conclusions. Other colleagues may pose as extroverts who excel in class discussions and easing presentations.

After you determine the various strengths of your colleagues, you can organize projects and team work based on each individual's personality strengths.

6. Managing conflicts effectively

If battle originates between yourself and the other coworker, make care to estimate the way you'd love to work during the scenario instead of responding in the heat of this moment.

Ask a personal meeting with another coworker and exhibit the truth in an objective method. Initiate a sensible conversation to talk about the dilemma of battle and find a mutually-beneficial alternative jointly.

Doing so will present your colleagues and your boss you are capable of managing emotionally-sensitive talks while maintaining a cool head.

7. Getting a 'yes' individual

Volunteer for new projects and specific missions. Be the very first person to put your hand up.

If your boss is seeking a person to measure, be the first to offer. It shows you are engaged and provides you with the chance to learn new abilities.

8. Saying 'no' when needed

This may appear contradictory to the prior stage, but that isn't!

If you are near burnout or possess a great deal happening in your own personal life, decide to say no more further work for those who need to.

Take note of your very own mental state of health. If you are incapable of carrying on longer, say no more instead of saying being not able to submit work.

If necessary, talk with your boss individually that you are not in the ideal place to undertake work however you plan to get back on the right track and once possible.

9. Showing humility

It is not feasible to be perfect in all all the time. In the event you make a mistake, own up to it.

Let your boss understand or coworker understand you made an error and you wish to fix it. Inform them that you've learned from the experience and you'll do things differently ahead.

Exercise humility so you might show a willingness to perform better.

10. Modeling work life balance

Make yourself maintenance a priority so you're devoting time from this workplace to your workout, nutrition and health objectives.

Carve out time after work to caring for you. Propose walking meetings throughout the daytime or try coordinating a group gym at lunch. Invite your colleagues to join you into attempting a new yoga course.

Prove your colleagues that you are dedicated to make life balance so you are able to appear as your very best self while on the job.

11. Under promise, over deliver

If you devote to finishing a job by a specific time, be sure you will get exactly what you said you are likely to do if you said you are likely to take action.

Do not commit to finishing a job employing an unrealistic time period. If you are not able to deliver, then you will necessarily damage your reputation and can negatively influence others' expectations of your skills.

Instead than committing to greater than you can achieve, dedicate to what you are capable of slightly less so you could over deliver on your promises.

12. Locating your own replies

Instead than turning into your colleagues or your boss whenever you have queries, do what you can to discover your own responses.

Inspection company policies, best practices and past circumstances. Use critical thinking to ascertain the way to best manage a situation and also demonstrate that you are in a position to make sound choices when it is demanded.

After doing your study, present the problem to your supervisor and discuss how you'd take care of the circumstance. Request advice to find out whether you're on the ideal path. In so doing you'll show ambition and drive.

13. Asking for assistance

If a situation arises that's over your pay-grade and you have to request help or advice, do this with humility.

Respectfully consult your supervisor or colleagues for their aid. Let them know which you're thankful for their help and they're prepared to talk about their understanding. Give to be of help to them whether it is needed later on and also repay the favor.

14. Offering assist

If it's possible for you to observe that a fellow coworker is fighting, offer to assist them out. Offering your aid will demonstrate your capability to function as a team participant.

If your office has already hired a new employee, offer to take them under your wing and show them the ropes. Let your supervisor know that you would be delighted to display them around.

It will show your seniority at work and also your interest in fostering morale and teamwork.

15. Accepting a brain break often

Require a couple of seconds every time you can to get a miniature meditation. From the restroom, the dining area, or on the subway on the way to operate, take a couple deep breaths and centre your mind.

Slow down your pulse and tune into your inner self. Inform yourself that function may be stressful but we all do not have to allow the stress change us. Return to the grounded and based state when you are feeling out of recovery.

How to be a thriving solopreneur

If you are not knowledgeable about the term 'solopreneur' however, and should you would like to produce financial and personal freedom in an uncertain market, now's the opportunity to understand what the term implies—and what it means to you.

Solopreneur

Definition: a self-employed individual who places their own hours, applies no other folks, and does not have any desire to market their small business.

Solopreneurs frequently function as authors, graphic designers, writers, photographers, entrepreneurs, advisers, coaches, coders, craftsmen, or any mix thereof. Most solopreneurs are trained and hold a minumum of one level in their disciplines. Nevertheless, the excellent matter is that solopreneurship is available to anyone who has worth to discuss (no matter the formal schooling), who is dedicated to optimizing their craft, and also that gets got the self-discipline to handle their time sensibly.

Benefits of this solopreneur lifestyle

The solopreneur lifestyle allows you to concentrate on the things you are most passionate about and also to boost your prices since you boost your value.—that is only the very first way it is far better than the usual 9-5. Should you request increases depending on the value you are bringing for your organization, or to do what you really love, they will fire you and replace you by somebody who does not understand their own worth—of that there are lots!

Being a solopreneur mechanically raises your own wealth, since wealth is the earnings multiplied by your optional time. When you operate at your home, you do not need to be concerned about two-hour commutes, you are able to holiday as frequently as possible, and you are able to take as many breaks as required to fulfill your own personal needs for health and pleasure—that usually means that you get to really be an individual. Thus, even in the event that you have a paycut to begin, you still have time to do the things you would like and to chase the things you are passionate about. That is what true wealth is. Because money cannot get back wasted moment.

Being per solopreneur also reduces the risk of being terminated or put off by 100 percent. With shaky trade relations along with also a borderline non-functional authorities, you can't if your 9-5 will probably be pulled away from beneath your feet.

Finally, solopreneurship educates you how you can promote yourself, the way to plan, and also the way to completely rely on your effort. Solopreneurship provides you accurate financial and personal freedom. It merely comes at the price of being more disciplined.

Who is interested in being a solopreneur?

Anyone may be thinking about being a solopreneur. Physicians, housewives, mothers, professors, students, dropouts, lawyers, young men and women, older men and women, old folks, folks who hate working for other folks, individuals who prize their own freetime—nearly anyone who does not need to forfeit their happiness and wellbeing to get a 9-5 job. The age group most related to solopreneurship now is that the millennial generation. We crave the function and liberty which simply cannot be seen in the conventional work environment.

Those who are not thinking about being a solopreneur normally have a fear of the unknown and have to be told exactly what to do with somebody else. Nevertheless, the actual question is that:

Who can really succeed because of a solopreneur?

This question is that the reason why millennial success exists. As a prosperous solopreneur (my customers vary from inc. 500 executives to ivy league grads) who had been a highschool expulsee, an army refuse as well as a school dropout, I am living proof that anyone may be a prosperous solopreneur regardless of their history, education or private history. Especially you.

However, you need to be ready to radically change the way you live just like I did. Because once you are by yourself, there is no one to save your butt or compensate for the lack of work.

You must be wholly accountable and responsible, which a lot of men and women are not eager to be. You need to be happy to work and find out more about your craft each and every day regardless of what you truly feel like. You need to get started looking for a balanced lifestyle which satisfies your requirements for health, enjoyment, fitness and goal—which means that you do not burn. And you need to be eager to get rid of the distractions, low-value customs and explanations * which keep you from making the most of your time and effort out of feeling sure enough to create amazing decisions daily.

(*you understand: being social websites 24-7, assessing your texts and emails daily, reading worthless posts and watching tv.)

Again, most people just are not eager to become this disciplined and also to require this much responsibility to their everyday decisions. They are too frightened to forego their creature comforts. However, if you're prepared, or whether you're prepared to understand how to style this lifestyle on your own, then that is the website. You'll learn what there is to learn about sustaining your solopreneur livelihood whilst getting a balanced and happy person in precisely the exact same moment.

Chapter one
How to become a solopreneur and lead an independent life

Solopreneur describes an individual that sets up and conducts a company by themselves. Who does not need to begin their own enterprise? I am rather sure that the majority of you at any stage in your lifetime have thought about constructing your personal fantasies.

There are a great deal of benefits for being a solopreneur for example fiscal freedom, comprehension, and versatility. But getting started since solopreneur could be hard.

Here are five suggestions to begin as a solopreneur and direct an independent lifestyle:

1. Select your fire

This is the most significant part your own solopreneur journey. You need to select something which you're really passionate about, since doing something which you don't enjoy on a daily basis will probably likely be exhaustive. A good deal of individuals run a company like it is a weight loss, and sooner or later they'll neglect.

There is a reason famous artists, musicians, artists, and authors earn a good deal of cash—they are very enthusiastic about it. Create a list of your hobbies then find out what's the 1 thing that you can perform on a daily basis without becoming tired. It may be anything such as painting, writing, or some other solutions you are able to provide.

Figure out how to decorate your own hobby or livelihood. Even though this is sometimes rough, I understand a chartered accountant that immediately began offering services on his own site after graduation rather than working under somebody. There may be a method in the event that you only sit back and think creatively.

"focus about building the greatest possible business enterprise. If you're good, people will find and chances will look."

2. Decide on a name

After you figured out that the market, the upcoming important step is to construct a brand around it. Nowadays building a new means getting online. Whether you are an artist or even a regional small business operator, you cannot discount the world wide web.

Select a suitable name which works for your market, start a site or website and make social networking profiles too. You do not need to devote a good deal of cash to construct a web site. Just be certain to increase your brand consciousness. In so doing you're minding your odds of becoming a profitable solopreneur.

If you carefully examine some regional tiny companies, you'll discover there's a massive difference in their new strategy in regards to online branding. If you are reading this, then I am fairly sure you have a particular degree skill-set to utilize technology; use the to maximize your brand awareness. As time passes, your brand provides you with an identity you will discover very happy.

3. Construct an appropriate program

You certainly do not need to quit your day job to begin your enterprise. A whole lot of people complain that they do not have plenty of time, but that is not the truth. They simply procrastinate without doing it.

Here is the key: there's not a single powerful person who left it they built it in balls. If you simply dedicate 1 hour daily to construct your fantasy, you'll have a very clear direction following a couple of months. Just be concerned about this "how" area and do it every day.

4. Construct a tiny team of salespeople

A solopreneur does not necessarily mean you've got to do everything. In reality, a great deal of successful solopreneurs possess a little group of freelance designers, programmers, attorneys, and proof readers.

After you achieve a certain amount of success, you are able to outsource some work to supply you with additional flexibility and time to consider. If a customer requires the logo to their site, I find several logo designers on outsourcing websites. Why? Because I am bad at designing but nevertheless offer you these solutions.

"none people is as smart as all people "

5. Fully dedicate yourself

It took me more than eight weeks to make my very first buck with my website, but after six decades here I am thinking—I am glad I did not stop. You will face a great deal of challenges, you may get tired, miserable and lack inspiration, however attempt to maintain a positive mindset towards your travels.

Consistently aim for long-term aims in life. Joel brown put a 10-year vision for achievement while beginning this site. Also, never get trapped using short term gains as it is a barrier for the own growth. Fully dedicate to your own dreams and think it is possible to generate a living with your fire and direct an independent life.

How to be a solopreneur

Whether you intend to handle your new company fulltime or you will continue to keep your day job for some time, here are a couple of actions that you can follow to enhance your odds of solopreneur achievement.

Many of those tiny start ups you visit today started out as multi-layer surgeries. An innovator has a concept and starts operating on it, normally in the comfort of a house office or kitchen table. Frequently that work has been performed over weekends and nights and after putting in full days in a daily job. Luckily, as a result of the numerous technician tools available now, you are able to readily get your thought well underway with nominal startup funds.

However, how can you begin? Whether you intend to handle your new company fulltime or you will continue to keep your day job for some time, here are a number of actions that you can follow to enhance your probability of solopreneur achievement.

Follow your fire

If you are starting a company simply to begin a company, you are starting off on the wrong foot. You need to find what you like doing and integrate that in your company concept, even if it's only a tool which talks to something you like. When you are enthusiastic about your goods, your clients, investors, and business partners will probably think passion, too. If you are an avid fisherman, then maybe your innovation is going to be a brand new program which aids your fellow amateurs locate the ideal fishing spot. If you like cars, your brand new company could centre about products that revolutionize how customers interact with their own automobiles.

Produce a vision

From the start, you ought to have a vision in your mind for your new firm. It's possible to integrate this vision in your business strategy when you are prepared, but largely it is crucial that you get it in mind while you're workingout. Your vision must consist of attainable targets that enable a decent time for finding where you need to be. Whenever you've got a strategy set up, you are more inclined to keep going as it appears there are simply too many hurdles.

Establish a budget

You will probably have all of the tools that you will need to begin, including the computer you have been utilizing for private endeavors. However, you'll eventually have to place money into advertising, product development, and traveling to conferences and media events. Set money aside while you can and place a budget set up for every one of the items so you'll know what to anticipate. This will inform you whether you are going to require financing, investment funds, or to spare more before you start your solopreneurship.

Automate

You do not need to become a master in bookkeeping, accounting, or job management to place these solutions to function in your small business. There are lots of technology tools available that can automate these procedures for a minimal fee. You will also require a system set up to collect information to your taxes in the conclusion of the calendar year, getting your expenses to permit you to pay off them to spend less in your tax invoice.

Do not attempt to do everything

As a solopreneur, you're be prepared to take care of all alone. This mindset will lead to burnout, as you can just sustain those anxiety levels for such a long time. Though your budget probably won't permit for many expenditures, spring for a outsource employee sometimes.

Drew hendricks out of infographics states"you might also have the ability to employ local college students as interns or rely upon friends and family for assistance in the first days. You could discover a buddy understands a graphic designer who'd really like to perform your emblem easily in exchange for having the ability to utilize it from his portfolio, as an example."

If you are considering starting your solopreneurship, a crystal clear vision and the ideal resources will point you in the ideal direction. Do not feel pressured to go fulltime immediately, but with some hard work on weekends and nights, in time you will probably find you are prepared to do this.

10 measures to turn into a solopreneur

In today's genuinely distributed planet, solopreneurship is a feasible route to choose for all. For prospective entrepreneurs, getting a solopreneur is a route to a fulfilling lifestyle concerning versatility, independence and control over your own fate.

But, it is not all rainbows and unicorns.

The fact is being a solopreneur means understanding how to live in what could be a remarkably difficult atmosphere. Creating a move for a solo entrepreneur entails gradually clearing a collection of catchy obstacles without falling tough across the way.

10 steps to be a solopreneur

In this bit, we will clarify what a solopreneur will be and have a look at the vital measures, in three overarching phases, that solopreneurs must go through to be able to flourish within the long term.

1. Settle on a company thought.

2. Do your own research.

3. Give it a title.

4. Exercise and test your own thought.

5. Set a budget.

6. Start building your new.

7. Make an internet presence.

8. Network with other people.

9. Consider automation.

10. Recall your own limits.

A solopreneur is basically a mix of 2 words: royal and entrepreneur. The expression is used to refer to somebody who runs and owns their company with no employees.

Even though solopreneurs operate their company independently, and they do occasionally hire builders or outsource specific jobs. This assists them up their time out of jobs outside their regions of competence or interest in order that they can concentrate on jobs which will assist them scale or grow their business further.

Solopreneurship is a fantastic selection for designers, copywriters, trainers, consultants, artists, illustrators and some other service provider who works with customers one-on-one. Nonetheless, it is possible to likewise be a solopreneur in case you sell handmade products and merchandise which are not mass-produced.

Now that we have found what a solopreneur will be, let us discuss the steps that you'll probably undergo to join the positions of solopreneurs.

Period 1: reaching lift off

He first point in your path to becoming a solopreneur is reaching lift off.

'Wantrepreneurs' are legion, the number of individuals who really muster the gumption to find something off the floor is considerably smaller.

To be honest, really achieving lift off isn't a trivial undertaking.

Most people do not have the luxury of history financing so as to ease in their new fact. For most, it is a matter of working double-time along with an present gig before the figures start consuming.

After you do really scratch together enough short term money, you are still facing a frightening leap into the unknown once you choose to really go to it fulltime.

In our roundup of all important phases for solopreneurs, attaining lift off can have a surprising number of courage, time and endurance.

If you are inside, keep shoving. If you are teetering on the border of it, then marshall your forces and get ready to become a brave new world.

In this point, you must settle on a company idea, confirm it, name, begin analyzing it, and earn a budget which can allow you to endure as soon as you're all set to move all in.

1. Settle on a company idea

Your travel to becoming a solopreneur begins with a good business idea.

But, it is not sufficient to just have a notion.

Your business idea ought to be contingent on something you are passionate about and will end up doing day in and day out for the near future.

But, additionally, it has to maintain demand, otherwise, your enthusiasm for it will not help you attain success.

Blend fire with need and you've got a profitable small business idea which can allow you to establish a company that is not just effective but it gets you eager to begin daily.

2. Do your study

After you understand your enterprise range, study your small business field so that you may really have a realistic notion about what it must have to succeed.

In particular, you are going to want to look closely at others in your area place their supplies, the way they market themand platforms they're active on.

The aim of the research isn't to replicate them but to provide you an overall idea about what is involved with conducting a similar business in addition to identify any possible gaps in the market you could fillout.

This step will even help you discover your limitations and narrow down exactly what you can and cannot do.

This is also the opportunity to work out your target market. You cannot (and do not wish to) be everything to most people.

Obtaining specific concerning the audience you aspire to function will lead to a whole lot more successful marketing and company operations.

Devote some opportunity to specifying the features shared with your perfect clients, such as:

1. Demographics

2. Professional specifics

3. Personality traits

4. Aims

5. Stress points / challenges

6. Buying procedure

With this data in hand, you can start to come up with thorough customer personas.

3. Give it a title

You likely got some thoughts while you're doing your study. Today, brainstorm more possible names on the new enterprise.

Be sure to look at the access to the corresponding domain as you restrict your list.

When you have finally settled on a title (which may require a little bit of time as it needs to, as it's significant), register the domain name.

Then, get an expert email address connected to a domain name. This will give credibility to a venture as you proceed along your journey to becoming a bonafide solopreneur.

4. Exercise and test your own thought

Strategy an hour per day to work on your enterprise and grow from that point.

A detox in low-value actions is a fantastic idea in this stage.

Forego mindlessly surfing social websites, binge-watching netflix or another action that will not transfer the needle in your small business.

Instead, exchange these low-value actions for being more productive to increase your individual enterprise.

5. Set a budget

The final step in this phase is to determine what goods, tools, services and other expenses you're going to want for your business enterprise. Then specify your financial plan.

As a general guideline, you are going to want to save six weeks' worth of living expenses until you choose your small business idea full moment.

Period 2: presence invention and media

Congratulations! You are currently at stage 2, which entails beginning to construct your brand, creating an internet presence, and networking with other people in your area.

6. Start building your new

"your brand joins the center of what you are promising to send to your clients to a pair of factors that remind the client of the assurance."

After you work out the character you want your new to value and the type of experience you would like your clients to have whenever they interact with you personally, you can start to create the visual strengths which will reflect your brand guarantee.

All these comprise:

· your emblem

· your brand colours

· your fonts

You also may look at developing a new design guide to pull it all together.

7. Make an internet presence

This point is the best time to set up your internet presence. You have already got a domain name and skilled email. You have developed the visual resources which reflect your brand. Now, it is time to construct a site which can allow you to share what you do, that you do it and how you do it.

Depending on the sort of business you are attempting to construct, a portfolio website may be helpful to showcase your previous endeavors. Including graphic designers, web designers, web designers, copywriters, illustrators, artists as well as some other creative small business market.

With designer templates for entrepreneurs in many different businesses, websites + marketing provides features such as:

1. The capacity to handle your site plus integrated advertising tools all in 1 place

2. Godaddy insight—data-driven hints and tailored action plans that will assist you keep enhancing your site and advertising campaigns

3. Customizable website topics—which makes it a snap to immediately change designs, fonts and colours

4. Built-in ssl certification

5. Reactive design

6. Speedy and reliable hosting

7. 24/7 customer suppor

Finally, do not neglect to enroll social handles which represent your brand and company name.

All of the above can allow you to place yourself as a skilled and allow you to build confidence with prospective customers and clients.

8. Network with other people

One of the very best methods to place yourself to the radar of possible customers would be to network with other folks.

Even if you are working alone, obtaining a solid network may be a large help.

Others can refer new customers to you when they're too active or when a customer isn't a fantastic match for them. And of course media can frequently cause collaborations which may place you in front of a fresh audience.

Period 3: consolidation and company

By this point, you are probably seeing the light at the end of the tunnel. You have been hustling to escape survival mode and also have attained some type of cruising altitude.

You have got dependable cash flow coming from, a secure client or customer base, and also a fairly good picture of the subsequent three to six weeks seem like. It is a huge aid to make it on this stage, but also the hard work is not over!

In the battle to have this much by yourself, it is very likely that you have assembled all manner of exactly what our programmer buddies would call"technical debt" across the way. That is a fancy method of stating that corners have been cut someplace.

At some point you are likely to need to manage the consequences—that is that point.

The first phases of getting an entrepreneur are basically sequential sprints, however nobody could dash forever—so it is time for another step.

9. Consider automation

This point is where you get started settling for a real marathon. It is about getting your ducks in a row and also simplifying down appropriate procedures and systems to radically enhance your productivity and profits.

Presenting automation in your company can free you from your minutiae of daily operations.

Automating certain procedures can improve your productivity by freeing between 2 and 3 work hours every day.

This can contain:

1. Establishing budgeting and/or bookkeeping applications

2. Setting up auto-deposits along with your lender

3. Employing social networking bots

4. Creating email trickle campaigns with autoresponders

Tools such as zapier, ifttt, automate.io and many others may join different programs and tools you are using in your company and manage a great deal of the administrative activities to you.

You may rely on them to automatically sync your own bills along with your bookkeeping applications, send a contract to register to new customers, produce a listing of your blog articles in a dictionary, and much more.

10. Recall your limitations

The most important consideration to remember is the constraints. Bear in mind that attempting to do or become all will result in burnout.

Concentrate on one major decision: can I outsource or hire?

For many solopreneurs in this phase of the sport, outsourcing particular projects or jobs is the thing to do. This frees you up to refocus your own time on tasks which can allow you to scale and grow your enterprise whilst saving the expenses related to hiring in-house workers.

Look to hiring a virtual assistant, and seek out strategic partnership opportunities inside your system.

It is about finding your own personal limitations, and working out the way to elegantly transcend them with the assistance of the others.

It is a wonderful spot to be. Get this much and down on the road, the world's your oyster!

Take another step and combine the solopreneur positions

Being that a solopreneur is far from a simple route to take, however, it provides outsized rewards for people who can take care of the requirements involved. Navigate your way through the vital phases we have outlined, and you're going to join a select group of those that are actually in charge of their working globe.

Let us briefly recap those vital steps :

Select a business idea you are enthusiastic about and establish your company range.

Conduct aggressive research and determine your intended audience.

Give your enterprise a title that reflects your offerings, and make sure you register the corresponding domain.

Validate and examine your thought so that you understand what it takes to achieve success.

Start small, decrease or remove low-value actions, and specify a budget to keep you afloat.

Function on building your new, such as your logo and other visual strengths.

Make an internet presence. Including building a successful site and promising your social websites manages.

Set a community to construct momentum and receive customers

Consolidate your place and receive super-organized, with the support of automation, as soon as you're on the first hump.

Contemplate the way to scale after you reach the limitations of your private capacity.

Why are you prepared to scale this specific mountain? Establish for solopreneur achievement using a site and built in advertising and marketing instruments that display all you've got to give.

Chapter two
Start working remotely

What exactly does it mean to work remotely

For most professionals looking to begin their remote professions, there is 1 notion holding back them—that which will distant work actually look like? It is only sensible to be fearful the lifestyle might not attract you. In reality, as fantastic as distant function is, it is definitely not for everybody.

Here is the first hand encounter on what this means to work so that you can tell whether it is the lifestyle for you or not.

You will function over you thought

When beginning their initial distant occupation, a lot of people believe that it is fun and games along with for the most part, they will do anything apart from work. In fact, remote workers work equally too much, and oftentimes, a whole lot more than people who sit at a workplace.

As it is difficult to put aside your operating environment from that in which you break and get fun, the reverse of slacking occurs. Many remote employees wind up doing work-related jobs beyond their operating hours to ensure an 8-hour work evening readily becomes 10 hours per day.

You will get to work for good businesses (or yourself)

As you start searching for your new (or initial) job, you would open a work board site and get started surfing through open places. Instantly, you're disqualify those that are hundreds of km away, unless you are eager to go to your occupation. But who is reassuring you will prefer the work as soon as you create such a large move? In the long run, this is much too risky of a project, which means that you settle for local occupations.

When working remotely, you're only limited by yourself. You're able to work for businesses from various cities, states, continents and time zones. If you are just beginning, you might not understand that advantages that bring, for example...

1. More choice in endeavors

2. Better paid occupations

3. More intriguing areas of work

4. More opportunities to find out

As an alternative, you can really go the freelance route and also operate yourself. When you've gained particular expertise, working as a freelancer is a wonderful alternative if you would like more liberty. But first make sure you get a steady source of earnings (stable paying customers on retainer), until you venture in to outsourcing. Moreover, make certain that you're knowledgeable about the intricacies of freelancing (discovering and pitching customers, sending suggestions, etc..)

You will need more free time

Before I started working remotely, I labored at a town roughly half an hour away from me. This meant about one hour every day of driving daily which has been basically lost in commuting. I might have spent the hour drinking coffee, playing tennis or studying. It wasn't till I had been gifted now which I understood I have a complete hour extra daily to do whatever I need. That is 5 hours every day, 20 hours every month.

A great deal of time that I could invest in any productive way which I desired. Due to working, a lot of men and women recover hours each month they squander travelling to and out of their workplace. I had been about the lower end of this scale also, as individuals who sail in bigger cities throughout the world need to fight through hours of visitors every day.

In addition, the 30-minute fracture supposed that I could jump by the kitchen and make myself something wholesome to eat, rather than stopping by in the fast food joint close to the workplace and going back and nearly never making it again in half an hour. Talking of food...

You will save money

Obviously, by spending money on gasoline, I managed to save considerable quantities in only a couple of months. But, there was still another price that popped up food and beverages. Since I was in the workplace, I purchased lunch and coffee.

Exactly like hours sitting in traffic, it stacks up over time. Maintaining up the numbers I spent each afternoon, it was that I had been spending tens of thousands of dollars each year on bites and beverages that I now keep convenient in the home.

I used the cash for my hobbies and also to purchase some presents for those people I adore. If you are operating from the workplace right now, have a fantastic look in your daily spending and you're going to learn precisely how much you could spare.

You will be glad... A lot

The harsh truth is that most distant employees spend massive quantities of time by themselves. Despite the fact that there are still co-working spaces, coffee stores, the fantastic outdoors and also the freedom to work from anyplace you would like, the great majority of individuals employed liberally operate by themselves, from the solitude of their property.

If you are the sort of person who enjoys the clamor and sound of a workplace, working remotely might be quite hard for you. A couple of decades ago as I started, the most bothersome thing was that the silence like I began functioning. There is no one to talk with, talk perform, drink some coffee... It becomes very lonely if you do not find ways to deal. As time passes, I have begun communicating more with coworkers via skype and slack and did not feel as left out like previously.

You will find occasions when you won't be alone... Regrettably

Request a distant worker in their greatest difficulty on the job and most will say that it is productivity that is taking a hit because they transferred from the workplace. The largest offender are distractions, and there is a number of if you are working at home.

Among my biggest issues is that I reside with my loved ones, and at the beginning, it was hard to describe the idea of distant work. This usually means that i'd frequently get upset as I use asks to assist, somebody asking me to perform something, and generally speaking, it had been rather tricky to stay focused. Colleagues who have kids have experienced bigger difficulties being left alone for a couple of hours per day to complete their continuing tasks.

Are you wishing to begin working damn? We all know that it is tough to locate a fantastic job board aimed especially at distant workers. That is precisely why we began anomadic, somewhere to join reputable businesses with workers searching for distant work. Join us now and discover your dream distant job!

Strategies for working liberally

For many professionals that sit in a workplace under fluorescent lighting daily, working from home seems like a fantasy. You have to ditch the sail and recover an excess hour of sleep. You do not need to pack dinner, also you're able to produce your coffee as strong as you would like. You are able to chill with your furry friend daily and pick the children up from school. But you may even stay on your pajamas or sweats (unless you've got a video phone).

However, the reality is, working at home is not always as simple as it may seem. It takes intentionality and a rigorous set of principles—at least initially.

So in the event you have accepted your very first remote job! Odds are, you are likely to enjoy operating remotely—it only requires a while. That is why it's very important to utilize these two work-from-home suggestions to put up yourself for success through your first week of telecommuting.

Strategies for working liberally

1. Address the reality that you'll be sitting... A lot

Oh, you believed you're sitting a good deal at your workplace job? Odds are, you're sit more when you are working remotely. "people spend more hours in their computer when they did at the workplace. Individuals was no more getting around interact, take telephone calls, or even visit meetings. "they want a much better job installation and also to get myself from the seated posture more frequently."

There are a couple of straightforward techniques to fix this dilemma: place a timer on your own telephone to remind yourself to stand up and stretch every hourinvest at a fitbit, that will buzz once you have been sitting for too long; or just take regular walks (with or without a puppy).

And regardless of what you do, do not work from the bed or sofa. You are simply asking for some severe neck and back problems.

2. Master the organization's tools and technology

After you have figured out how your work station and the best way to keep yourself from becoming too exhausted, it is time to learn your institution's tools and technology. This is particularly important once you're working out of home because you can't tap on your co-worker about your shoulder to ask queries.

Require your time browsing the organization's training records and onboarding stuff. Walk through every new instrument—particularly those which revolve about communication and workflow—play with them. You may even hunt for further tutorials on the internet.

Dedicating longer on this through your first week can allow you to save time and prevent communication snafus down the street.

3. Set a strict program for yourself (at least originally)

Working remotely will imply more versatility, which is harmful whatever your workforce. That is why it's crucial that you decide on a rigorous structure to your daily life, particularly when you're first beginning.

"start strict on your own," sanders guides. "it is more difficult to build much better customs as soon as you've established poor ones. I moved to this being hyper-aware that I was able to get behind quite easily if I am not realistic"

The first portion of the routine should centre around customs outside your job duties: wake up, get dressed, make breakfast, brew a pot of coffee, and listen to your workspace. At lunch, program time to escape from the desk and then eat a hearty meal. Perhaps even select a fast run in case you've got enough time. The next portion of the routine should centre around your workouts. Produce listsset your goals for every day, and adhere to your deadlines.

"i structure my day all over the activities I want to get done. I would like to have them done inside my regular eight- day to nine-hour afternoon," sanders explains. When he gives himself a lot of idle, he will lose his most effective hours of this afternoon, so he will be stuck working when he is exhausted.

4. Produce links with co-workers, even from afar

For a few, working at home can boost productivity. After all, you do not possess the typical off-the-shelf distractions (ahem, co-workers). On the flip side, you may feel isolated—as if you are operating in a vacuumcleaner.

Since your organization allows remote employees (or functions completely distant) it probably utilizes a communication software such as slack, microsoft teams, or even google hangouts. Take advantage of these programs to communicate with your teammates, even if it is not constantly work-related.

Sanders' team employs slack. 1 station is dedicated to function talks, while some other channel is only for pleasure. There, they will share anything they need, from what they failed over the weekend into kitty images. Though it's your first week the job, do not be scared to donate to a station similar to this. Share your favored meme, a photograph of your puppy or kitty, or perhaps throw into a cheesy icebreaker.

"which was a lifesaver," sanders says. "it is less isolating. Even when you're not face- to- face, you are still interacting"

5. Require measures to detach and place work-life boundaries

You may be astonished just how simple it's to turn into a workaholic when you are operating remotely. You wake up, open your notebook, and get started pushing to reach your deadlines. Before you know it, the hours have thrown away and you inadvertently skipped lunch and almost missed dinner.

At 11 p.m., as you are eventually unwinding, you obtain a slack notification requesting for an extra document. The sender may not mean that you reply straight away, but you also cannot quit thinking about it, which means that you get back in your own pc. Before you know it, you are feeling profoundly burnt out.

Fortunately, there are a couple methods to prevent this from occurring:

Stick into the rigorous pattern you generated which balances both your requirements and your business's needs.

Establish boundaries along with your co-workers. If you are working for a business which works on no set program, speak what hours you will normally be online.

Use the business workflow and communication tools to your benefit. List the common hours you are on line and available for dialog, muting your alarms through your off hours.

6. Know your co-workers' communication tastes

Just like you've got your personal tastes, your co-workers may also. Since you can know them, get to understand their communication and work preferences. If you would like, ask these questions upfront:"do you like me to message opinions directly for you or place them at the file?" "when I have questions, how do you like for me to guide youpersonally, or would you would like to establish a brief time to check out?"

You may also take notes along the way because you start to work together and find out in their workouts.

7. Be an advocate on your own

When you are working remotely, you may need to be intentional about looking for feedback from the supervisor. At the workplace, it's simple to stop from the supervisor's desk and inquire how what is searching or ask a query. On the internet, which needs a message, telephone call, or movie chat.

Odds are, you're set up a week or biweekly one-on-one meetings with your supervisor. That is the ideal time to assess in and solicit comments or ask questions. If, however, you feel like you are drifting out at a void, do not be afraid to get in touch with your supervisor.

When started working remotely, folks was really navigating new function for a manager. "i appreciated if I had someone who'd come to me saying,'i believe I am doing ok, but could I get any comments?'"

Do not be scared to talk and be your personal advocate.

8. Have a backup plan

At this stage, you ought to be feeling quite great about your first-week working distant. You have got your workspace, your regular, your own list of prioritiesyour communication stations... But do not get too cluttered.

It is time to deal with some what-if situations: what if your electricity goes out? Imagine if the net goes down? Imagine if you simply aren't able to concentrate to save your own life? Imagine should you can do is stare in your bed whilst longing for a rest?

All these events will happen, therefore have a backup plan set up. Whether your kid's outside or you are just listless, understand where it is possible to go out of your home or apartment to do the job. Locate your go-to coffee store, a co-working area with ample hours, or even your closest library. You will thank yourself if the net's down and you have a meeting within 10 minutes.

9. Keep your social life beyond work

Finished your very first week to the new occupation? Congratulations! Invite your buddies to happy moments, catch dinner with your spouse, or visit the playground with your loved ones. Now that you are a fulltime remote worker, you're going to want to locate explanations to socialize with people rather than, well, your own pc.

6 measures ways to acquire a remote desktop job (ultimate guide)

Obtaining a distant project. It seems like a fairly viable target in 2020 today, right?

More comfort with your program. No longer sitting in traffic driving to the workplace. More time to devote towards unwanted jobs. The list of benefits goes on and on...

As a full-time freelancer and consultant, I expect to experience a number of these added benefits. However, being in company fulltime for yourself also will come with more dangers, higher prices, and also the ever-present possibility of down times.

Assessing out ways to acquire a distant job that you'll like, can rather be a rather delighted medium between the 2 extremes of self-employment and spending 10 hours each day in a workplace which drains your energy.

Obtaining a distant job can really be perfect for analyzing your way to self-employment—watching how nicely you'd handle your own time, remain inspired and effective working at home, coffee shops or even a co-working area. Nowadays, countless men and women are landing distant tasks for all these reasons (and more).

The application procedure for distant tasks may appear a bit confusing, but it is really much tougher than a standard application procedure, only different.

Now, let us begin.

1. Ask yourself if obtaining a remote job is really suitable for you.

Before we receive entrenched in really landing a distant job, we will need to chat about whether remote is perfect for you especially. This component requires some study and self-reflection.

For example, distant function is an amazing match for my private way of life and work design, for these reasons:

1. I am unashamedly, but I receive a great deal of in-person interaction with friends outside work.

2. I enjoy speaking to people. Discussing the telephone or through video chat suits my requirement for in-person communication as much as real, in-person communicating.

3. I am also a big runner, and now that I like spending time with my loved ones.

4. I like my job, I don't have any difficulty concentrating, and I am ready to rip myself out of work once I am done for this day.

If you wish to leap into distant work together with both feet, so it is crucial that you ask yourself whether the pros outweigh the disadvantages. For me personally, there was important upsidedown, and it had been a no brainer to move distant and carry on work from home tasks. For one the story may differ.

We have recorded the pros and disadvantages of working out of house below. Consider these through the lens of your very own ideal way of life, and also the lens of that which makes you productive.

11 pro's and con's of getting a remote desktop job

Experts of obtaining a remote desktop job:

1. No rush: your dreaded commute is over, no longer visitors or bothersome rush hour metro rides

2. Your schedule: no one is watching. Wish to see netflix at 11:00 a.m. On a monday? Go ahead, nobody will understand. Based upon your job function, you are able to work if you would like to.

3. Function anywhere: it is possible to get the job done literally everywhere. I operate on my backpack when it is nice out, however, a few people decide to operate in another country every month or two.

4. Family period: for those who have children (or a set of cavalier king charles spaniels) you will have more time to hang together. Evidently, you do not need them to invade your own workspace, however, function flexibility allows for much more household (or puppy) time.

5. Prices: commute prices are nil. You can even say goodbye to 13 fries for lunch and then say hello into the supermarket to get a less expensive lunch and breakfast.

6. Office pressure and distractions: nobody is quitting from the table and deflecting you out of work. No office play with distant work.

Sounds fantastic right? Not too quickly, there are some drawbacks to working remotely:

Disadvantages of obtaining a remote job:

1. Loneliness: I had someone tell me this "functioning at home is a fantastic way toward despair". I really agree. Working 5 days each week entirely alone could get lonely.

2. Overworking: appears like underworking will be the issue here...correct? In fact, more individuals struggle to split household life and work, leading to an never ending job day. Burnout gets quite real, extremely fast, should you encounter poor work habits in your home.

3. Underworking: depending upon your character, in general job seeker, and enjoy for the project function, productivity may actually drop at a distant atmosphere. If direct oversight motivates you to get work, working at home may destroy your motivation.

4. No more"water cooler minutes": many say that imagination and innovation can occur at impromptu moments on the job. Being close to colleagues generates more social communication. A number of those moments are dropped with distant work.

5. Restricted team social actions: some organizations are partly distant. By way of instance, perhaps only 10 percent of the work force is distant. When

everybody goes to get a joyous hourand another distant team members may be too much off to combine. Feelings of seclusion ensue.

Remote work isn't for all, some individuals actually flourish in a workplace environment, and many others flourish working remotely.

I have talked to some folks that attempted distant work and immediately realized they want more peer pressure interaction. I have talked to some other individuals who ended up back at the workplace since they just want somewhere to go daily.

2. Ascertain what truly motivates you.

Taking a distant job is practically like being the entrepreneur, and also inspirational quotations alone will not fuel you eternally.

No one is on your shoulder telling you to perform your work. With distant function, the single man telling you to operate is that you.

With a distant task, the single man telling you to operate is that you."

Now that you understand the advantages and disadvantages of having a distant job, it is time to do a little bit of self-reflection.

The best remote employees actually love their job and enjoy what they create. If you do not love what you do, then your mattress abruptly becomes really comfy—especially if nobody is telling you how to wake up and move.

Most people today begin to find this sense of dread sunday nights for just one reason or the other. Should you get this feeling, examine it. If you despise being in consumer success in the workplace, you're likely going to hate being in consumer success in your home also. If you'd like your job however the sunday fear comes from the strain of flying, you may be a fantastic match for distant work.

I personally anticipate mondays (frankly) since I love everything I do, and also that I get to do exactly what I enjoy from home.

Having a distant project is an wonderful chance to live the life you need while performing the job that you like. Just be certain it's a match for you before hitting the distant task boards.

3. The way to locate your fantasy remote job.

If you are still reading, you are probably prepared to storm the digital gates of this distant work-world. Nonetheless, if you would like to acquire a distant job... You will first have to understand where to search.

The very best websites for finding great remote jobs.

Most job websites do not have an extremely great"remote work" filter, which normally contributes to hours of sifting through freelancer jobs and other gigs which may not be the ideal fit. Each the project boards under do the sifting for you and attribute especially distant tasks:

In our expertise, all these are hands down the best websites for finding distant tasks:

1. Flexjobs.

This website provides fulltime, part-timejob, and also some tasks that are ideal for analyzing your way to starting an independent business. Businesses can post jobs at no cost, but applicants need to pay $14.99 per month for the support. Honestly, the $14.99 is a little price to pay to get access to the job opportunities they bill. Personally, I know some people who have developed a stance through flexjobs.

External of the paid support, in addition they have a great deal of free tools for distant job seekers. The majority of the other websites I will discuss attribute"jobs in technology", however flexjobs provides job postings from a vast array of businesses. Bonus: flexjobs has new articles all of the time, and graphics typically return to you immediately after you have implemented.

2. Angellist.

I have personally acquired work out of angellist. There is no commission and fresh job postings are added every day. Contrary to the other websites on this listing, this website is geared especially toward start-ups. If you would like to work from an early stage startup, then this is where to be. There's not any charge to utilize angellist, but you will want to earn a profile. Your profile is the resume so make sure it stands out.

You get interviews by clicking on"yes, I am curious" and by simply leaving just a little note for your hiring supervisor. If the business likes your profile, then they will establish a meeting with you. The procedure with angellist is super simple, no resume or cover letter required. I have implemented and obtained a response in a couple of hours, and every job posting informs you if the work poster has been last"busy". Guru tip: stay far in the"busy 2 months back," or afterwards.

3. Hubstaff talent.

On hubstaff, you also have the choice of looking for distant projects that are fulltime, hourly freelancer contract, and also fixed cost—this particular platform is very great if you are seeking to take on freelance job to enhance your earnings. Using their countless open functions which range from internet development, to layout, advertising, sales, client assistance, social networking marketing and much more, there is something for everybody with this distant job stage.

4. Pangian.

When you combine pangian, you are tapping into among those most popular online communities rather than just finding remote tasks, but also for linking with fellow distant employees that are located in over 121 countries from all over the globe. While their distant job board boasts more than 12,897 tasks from 312 businesses, the system's real magic lies inside their close-knit neighborhood and chat conversation where you are able to swap distant working hints and learn from one another.

5. Remote.com.

This website provides you access to a selection of start-ups to publicly traded businesses. Job seekers are able to apply free of charge if their profile fulfills the requirements for work. Remote.com also includes a 19 premium alternative for extra vulnerability. Have a look at their"firms" webpage and you're going to find some big names. In the event you choose to register for remote.com they will allow you to find the reimbursement for tasks before you apply.

I also love remote.com since they post numerous occupations. Should you check daily, they will typically install 4-5 tasks from 1 new firm. Remote.com articles get very good reaction times, many will respond in just a day or 2.

6. Remote.co.

Remote.co (maybe not remote.com) is really a part of flexjobs, however, provides some extra job postings. I am placing this website on the record due to the resources. They post projects every day (and excellent jobs at the), and also their"firms" site is an awesome place to find out about businesses which hire distant employees.

If you do wind up using for work, the answer time is very similar to that of a normal job program. They have excellent blog tools along with an faq section for distant job seekers. The job posting grade is great, but this is a wonderful place to find out about operating remotely.

7. Weworkremotely.

This is almost just a work board, however, a fantastic job board for distant jobs. There's not any program fee, along with the website is actually simple to navigate. 1 drawback here's slower program reaction times (not certain why).

Most of the tasks are concentrated on applications engineering/ design, however this really is a daily-checker if you're on the distant job search. When I am on the lookout for a distant task, I make certain that you test weworkremotely to get sure.

8. Jobspresso.

This website is just another"check regular" task board. They've postings from a number of the greatest names in distant work, plus they place new tasks daily. I enjoy jobspresso since they have a large volume of occupations, plus they post frequently. Not a great deal of job hunting resources, but after these twitter is a very wonderful way to keep up with postings.

Having looked for distant work in the not too distant past, these sites have afforded some fantastic chances. I have had good experiences with all the above mentioned businesses, however I cannot say the exact same for the sites below. Here are some websites that are bad for distant work:

The worst websites for finding remote jobs:

1. Linkedin.

Perhaps a surprise? Linkedin is your largest professional community and possibly the ideal spot to discover a job... But it is not the ideal location to discover a distant job. I will give them some credit: they've been incorporating more distant jobs recently. However, generally speaking, remote tasks are tough to discover, and they frequently wind up being in-house jobs.

Looking for an on site job? Linkedin is also your very best option. But distant? You are going to be sifting through tasks for hoursand if you eventually locate the needle-in-the-haystack remote occupation, the project poster has generally made a error. You'll come across the occupation isn't distant or the organization isn't too desirable. In case you've got boundless hours for job hunting, you may come across a couple distant jobs in this case, however, these very same tasks are often posted on a few of the suggested distant job boards.

2. Really.

My beef this is largely around wasted moment. There are in fact a reasonable number of remote tasks on really, and they're simple to discover, but a great deal of these are place specific or not distant in any way. The distant companies on really can be funny at times also. If you're seeking a distant job in technology, this really isn't where to search.

But, i'll say that really does provide distant jobs in businesses outside technology. For my planned job hunt (i have worked in technology), this area turned into a dud. If I was searching for employment out tech, perhaps not. Overall—that the postings are peppered with bizarre businesses and non-remote tasks, disguised as distant jobs. So my badge of disapproval.

3. Monster.

This is just right up not the location for distant tasks. I really don't believe that they concentrate on itand it reveals. They seldom post remote tasks, and if they do, the tasks are often place specific or using an unknown business. I believe dragon is a great spot to locate a non-remote occupation, but it is not worth your time to hunt here for distant openings.

Depending in your skill set and business expertise, among the advised distant job boards may be more precious than others. For me especially, angellist was enormously useful. I used it to locate work in a small technology startup in a sales ability. When I had another job role or distinct business expertise, i'd start with flexjobs. They have good technology openings, but in addition they support a range of businesses.

There are additional distant job sites, but regardless of what business or job role you are searching on, the 6 cited previously would be the very best places to get started.

4. Know exactly what remote employers are searching for.

The vast majority of distant employers are searching for two chief items: (1) trusted folks and (2) those who love their job.

I state because micromanagement is passing for distant businesses. Remote companies will need to trust that every team member is going to perform their job, and also make high quality work.

"remote companies want trusted people who enjoy their job."

When you land your initial distant interview, do not be shocked if your interviewer appears to be very interested to speak about you as a individual. Diversity is appreciated. You may be communication with group members at san francisco, bombay, london, and mexico city at precisely the exact same moment. Should you spend some time working on a private site, or want to travel and kitesurf on weekends, then do not hold that info back. In a distant interview, do not be scared to be you. Side note: in case you would like to construct your abilities as a blogger, then begin with those blogging classes from the world's best experts now.

I hate when folks tell me "just be yourself"—however in distant interviews, dialing the corporate talk and behaving like yourself makes you even trustworthy. I have discovered that many of remote employees (distant hiring supervisors) appear to, for whatever reason, have greater emotional intelligence than normal. They will have the ability to tell if you're being genuine.

I talked about self-reflection just a bit sooner: here comes a little additional inner thinking.

External of hiring trustable men and women, remote businesses need people who are enthusiastic about what they're doing.

If you're obtaining a distant job simply because you hate your job, and you are trusting that working from home can help...regrettably, it will not. Working at home may make it more difficult.

Working from house provides myriad great distractions. Your tv may be calling your name, along with your dog may be calling your name daily. If you are not motivated to operate, you probably won't function if nobody is looking over your shoulderagain.

Remote work is earmarked for people who enjoy, or really like what they're doing. Seems harsh, but your motivators will need to be in the perfect location.

Should you reveal your distant interviewer just how much you really care about your job, I guarantee, it is going to resonate together.

To caution: be real and show enthusiasm for your job (one approach to show that curiosity would be to begin a website, discuss smart blog post thoughts on your area and finally even earn money blogging). Now that you're ready to pinpoint the skills part of this interview, a few challenging skills are essential for functioning remotely:

Remote organizations are searching for problem solvers. This may come in the shape of startup expertise, entrepreneurial expertise, internally advanced individuals (intrapreneurs), or just plain additional distant work experience.

Why do they desire this adventure? Since there'll come a time at which you'll possess a query, and your complete company may be unavailable. They will want you to be flexible, and capable of solving problems by yourself.

When I worked at a office, my supervisor was at the cubicle across from me personally. When there was a crisis, I might run into her say, help!

To be obvious, slack and other communication programs exist because of this. You likely will not be abandoned to the wolves frequently. But distant organizations are searching for autonomous employees. From the interview process, prepare yourself to talk about your autonomous job experience.

Do not believe you've got autonomous work expertise? Do not worry, no one actually does... Unless you have worked liberally or started your own company before. Time for creative.

I began an e-commerce business for a negative hustle few decades back. I worked when I got home from my day job. Additionally, I had a painting provider in school where I went door to door selling painting solutions. All that reveals my self-starter encounter.

5. Create a resume for a remote job program.

Self-starter experience goes a very long way in a meeting. However, to acquire an interview, your resume has to be tailored to distant businesses. Listed below are a couple of items to put in your resume that will allow it to stand out to distant employers (and yet another exceptionally helpful resume builder to test out):

Talk about resources: remote businesses utilize applications to bridge the communication gap. List any applications tools which you're familiar with using. Some may comprise: slack, salesforce, basecamp, trello, harvest, gotomeeting, google hangouts, skype, zoom, zapier, and a lot more.

Communication: communication begins with your resume. Remote businesses fail due to terrible communication, so they seem to employ incredible communicators. Your resume must chat about your communication abilities, and typos ought to be non-existent. Your email communicating with hiring managers and recruiters ought to be good also, and it cannot hurt to say you'll take your cybersecurity badly as a distant employee also.

Innovation or portfolio: should you've done some thing to innovate work, place that in your resume. In case you've got a portfolio, talk about that also.

Negative jobs: determined by the way you breach this topic, side jobs can begin some controversy. You may not wish to place those jobs front and centre in your resume unless it provides into a situation, but you will want to chat about them in a meeting. Working on a job autonomously proves that you take motivation. I say tread softly since some companies, distant or not, may believe your side job will take away time from the day job.

Location: this might appear obvious, however when a distant job is place specific, be certain that you mention your closeness to this place. By way of instance, some sales endeavors may have an nyc land. Should you reside in nyc, be certain you mention it on your own correspondence with the business.

Outcomes: in case you have any hard numbers connected with your work, place those on the restart also. By way of instance, when you've got the marketing abilities and also you doubled visitors in x time period, as a result of x motives—that is great resume advice.

Autonomy: cannot hurt to chat any moment you had been a "self-starter" or functioned on deliverables without a lot of supervision. Any moment you worked with reduced or no oversight is invaluable. Your capacity to operate autonomously is large, however you do not have to have direct distant experience to operate remotely.

"remote work is focused on implementation."

Working liberally is more outcomes concentrated than hours-worked concentrated. Some distant positions will need 9:00-5:00 work, while others will not whatsoever. Some distant companies will not track your hours, but they will be tracking your deliverables.

If you adore your job, you are a real individual, and also you tailor your resume into distant businesses. You are on the ideal path to landing a distant job.

6. Bringing it all house (no pun intended).

One last suggestion before you reach on the distant job boards: pick up a copy of remote. I simply discovered the book to offer fantastic insights to working remotely.

For remote job seekers, the publication outlines how the fantastic distant company is handled and supplies you with a summary of things to look for in a distant employer.

With your reading record in hand, here is a recap of your activity items for obtaining a distant job:

1. Ascertain if distant is ideal for you personally (maybe you would be content where you have a boost?).

2. Consider the pros and cons, and also understand your personal motivators.

3. Know that the ideal websites for distant job searching.

4. Know the worst websites for distant job searching.

5. Get knowledgeable about the distant community.

6. Be mindful, be sovereign, and enjoy your work.

7. Tailor your resume for distant job applications.

8. Take your job hunt in your own hands.

When you do eventually get a distant job, it may look odd at first... Working for a business free of hq, or even a business with an hq tens of kilometers apart. Give it a couple of weeks and you're going to feel right at home (literally).

Honestly, on my very first day of distant work, although I had been waiting to satisfy my new supervisor on the seminar lineup, it crossed my mind that the entire company may not even be actual.

I had this flash of stress that the entire thing was bogus! Then the assembly began and my own supervisor and I put working. Working remotely and communication remotely isn't more difficult, or much more complicated than any other occupation, it is simply different.

"obtaining a distant job isn't any more challenging than a standard job, it is just different."

The same could be stated for landing a distant job. The job application isn't harder, it is just somewhat different. Should you immerse yourself at the distant community and show enthusiasm for your job, you're guaranteed to distinguish yourself from other distant job seekers.

Great luck getting these distant job programs on the market. Remote work was rewarding for me, it matches with my working design, and that I could not be more happy writing this article in my backpack on a bright day.

New to distant working? Do not make these errors

Working remotely offers individuals a world of advantages, which explains why so many are keen to embrace a hierarchical arrangement. However, doing your work out of a conventional office setting requires some getting used to, and should you go in vain, you might wind up fighting or perhaps damaging your livelihood in the procedure. With that in mind, here are 3 remote workouts mistakes you need to make an effort to prevent:

1. Getting too easily distracted

Make no mistake about itdistractions are typical in workplace environments, if they arrive in the kind of loud gear, perpetually ringing telephones, or even chatty coworkers. But working remotely will come with its host of distractions. In the event you choose to set up shop at a nearby coffeehouse, then you are able to readily get chucked off your rhythm from the continuous bustle of folks coming in and outside. You could also be tempted to strike up conversations, particularly in the event that you begin to miss the camaraderie of workplace life.

Working from home, you're going to be face to face with all the heap of private email from the preceding week which never got thrown, the laundry which desperately wants to get done, the dirty breakfast dishes, or even the tv enticing one to have a rest.

To combat these distractions, and identify your largest possible causes, and engineer your own surroundings in a way which can allow you to prevent them. By way of instance, in the event that you normally work out of your living space, you may go as far as to set the tv remote someplace at the home, or have your partner conceal it, to keep you from falling prey to the desire to turn it around and knock off. Oryou may pledge to just handle your laundry between jobs as a psychological rest of sorts—but only once you have checked a variety of key work things off your record.

2. Not setting boundaries

You would think a distant arrangement would contribute to a greater work-life equilibrium, but when you are not careful, you can end up in the contrary circumstance. This particularly applies if you are typically doing your work from your home. The motive? Whenever your private area and your office area will be the exact same area, the temptation to do"one more thing" work-wise is obviously there. That may make it a battle to rip yourself away from the work, even sometimes when you are not predicted to be around the clock.

The alternative? Map out a program which defines if you will and will not be operating. Grantedyou might bend the rules here and there if office crises attack, but placing apparent working hours means you are going to be less inclined to allow your task take over a lot of your lifetime, a scenario that could result in you burning.

3. Not having the ideal setup

Placing up store in the corner of the kitchen or in a corner of your bedroom may appear to be a fantastic idea initially. But should you realize that you are missing the vital tools you require, or you don't have sufficient space to spread out, you may immediately begin peeling your distant arrangement.

Therefore, evaluate your distant work space choices before you bidding farewell to the workplace. Ensure that you are able to supply yourself with a sensible atmosphere for getting your work done. If, as an instance, a part of your project entails comparing different site designs, you will probably wish to be certain that you've got a table or desk that is big enough to support many screens. You might require a dedicated area to put away documents and supplies. The crucial thing is to exercise your installation appropriately beforehand, to be certain that it's acceptable for all your requirements. If not, you risk becoming frustrated—or worse, more derailed.

Working liberally could be a positive experience in lots of ways. Just make sure you get around the beginner mistakes which will make you regret taking a rest from workplace life.

Chapter three

12 things you didn't intend for as you launched hiring remote workers

Remote work is rising. Are you prepared?

Think it or not, distant work has increased by 140 percent since 2005, almost 10x faster than the remainder of the work force. In reality, over 4.3 million workers (3.2percent of the job) currently work at home at least half time based on international workplace analytics.

With the rapid growth in price of living in several cities, together with new technology which makes distant work simpler, you can anticipate this trend to continue to develop for a long time to come.

Regrettably, there is more to distant work compared to individuals not coming in precisely the exact same workplace as you. Possessing distant team members has unique challenges, both for supervisors leading those workers, and also for the workers themselves. Most managers are not ready for it, since they do not understand how different it truly is.

Together with those struggles, there are a number of truths connected with distant work which may influence your preferences when selecting your very first remote workers.

For example, the concept that remote employees are electronic nomads traveling with their own laptop, working around the shore, is completely false; as distant operate evangelist and former cto of product hunt, andreas klinger, commented on twitter:

Instead, the majority of the countless distant workers work at house, a co-working area, or discuss a fulltime workplace. They likewise don't travel over the ordinary worker.

12 challenges you did not strategy for as you started selecting remote workers (and what to do in these)

The lighthouse staff is distant, and we have been talking with various distant leaders throughout the past couple of months, amassing both private and public tales regarding the challenges unique to getting remote workers.

Consider these protect rails that will assist you avoid making the very same errors other leaders have left. Some may boost morale and effective, though some will save you tens of thousands of dollars by preventing unexpected fines and taxes!

1) handling time zones to your remote workers

Dealing with distinct time zones is among the initial challenges you experience when dealing with remote workers.

Little differences, such as the 3 hours that different california and new york, are not frequently that big of a deal. But, crossing seas changes which in a huge way.

For example, the us west coast (pdt) into israel is a 10 hour time gap (and the latter do not operate fridays). If you are in silicon valley and you are messaging a staff member in israel very first thing on your morning, then they are probably already from the workplace to the day. Plus they will not be in however from the end of the day.

With a program like this, occasionally you will eliminate an whole day of work for a response or to get a dialogue, simply because of time zone differences.

This may work out good for many emails and a few messages, however it makes it extremely hard for scheduling team meetings. Less overlap in time zones also signifies when they will need to speak to someone live, that person might not be accessible.

The tyranny of the primary business time zone

All these problems can make an irregular power lively for extended distance distant employees. When a remote worker is lots of time zones apart from the majority of your staff, they could face numerous challenges

To generate a generally approved assembly period, thello might need to get up really early, stay up really late, or even overlook things like average family time.

Remote employees might be excluded from encounters with explanations used for example, "we had to make a decision fast" or even "their own window of assembly times is currently complete."

They can completely alter the hours that they operate, making them sleep considerably differently compared to partners, friends, and acquaintances.

2) recognizing intention from distant communication

We ought to "presume ignorance before malice," when communication with other individuals.

We can often provide folks the benefit of the doubt based on an assortment of nonverbal cues and signs such as a grin, the inflection of their gender, or their overall posture.

We possess eons of programming inside usway back from our ancient days of success, made to pick up on a number of these non-verbal signals—hints that you cannot pick up on in case you cannot see somebody face-to-face.

As a result, once we speak on line, via slack, email, or remarks within a project management tool, it is too easy to assume the worst of our staff members out of some drawback sounding message.

Our head is executing a automatic defense software which never before needed to draw conclusions with such restricted data. While this occurs, everybody on your team endures.

The way to enhance remote communication: have routine video forecasts

You can't and should not quit texting distant team members. But 1 thing you can do to assist this dilemma would be to get routine video calls. Anyone handling remote workers for quite a very long time will inform you that is remote control 101.

Tools such as zoom and google hangouts create this easier than ever before. The continuing progress in video conferencing technologies usually means the annoying bugs of recent decades are thanksfully getting less and less frequent.

It is also reasonable to anticipate your remote workers to work someplace they are able to have high bandwidth net, to ensure connectivity is never a barrier for communicating. It's possible to test for this through the interview procedure, by seeing just how simple it's to get quality video calls together throughout the interview procedure.

Most importantly, utilize video as far as possible!

Attempt to create every one on team and one meeting a movie call. Doing this will provide you back a lot of the formerly lost nonverbal communicating: their own voice, their tone, and their own body language.

It also generates opportunities to build greater rapport together and for all to get to know each other much more, such as when I watched a coworker sporting a mark price jersey and also afterwards amazed him with a connected present.

3) empathizing with distinct cultural communication styles

Past knowing a coworker's purpose, occasionally communication obstacles can occur whenever your remote worker is from another culture. What one person believes is acceptable and normal can feel strange, offensive, or overseas to a different individual.

Even inside the u.s., there are unique styles. By way of instance, new yorkers are famous for being brash and guide, while socal people are frequently more direct and laid back.

Can you tell when someone is being a jerk, or they are simply being straight (sometimes they are the exact same thing)? There is a good deal of nuance to know in case you have not lived anyplace your distant workers possess.

The point is you might not even understand when you are breaking up, or maybe not getting through to somebody, and the exact same goes for the remote workers.

The only way to understand would be to take some opportunity to get to learn your distant employees well, also to make certain that there's a definite, open conversation together. You have to ask great questions in the beginning such as those recommendation on comments:

1. How can you like comments—the moderate (irc, email, in person, etc..)

2. How can you enjoy feedback—regular such as in 1:1s, or even as-it-happens

3. How can you want to get recognition? (private or public)

Learning these items can allow you to begin on a stronger base together. Afterward, over time you are able to find out more about their civilization, and discuss a few of yours so you can understand each other.

Culture and customs affect everything

Realize but this goes beyond feedback and coaching. This may affect everything from the way that worker asks for a marketing, brings up problems, and complies with the remainder of the group.

It is important to take a while to know their cultural communication fashion and clarify yours. This way, you are not comparing them up from the very own cultural standards, and you're able to work together to bridge any breaks or misunderstandings.

In the conclusion, the responsibility will be shared with you and everyone in your staff to comprehend each other.

As you earn more and more civilizations across the world, lead by example and explicitly speak about how there could be instances individuals will misunderstand each other. In so doing, you're help everybody give each other the benefit of the doubt, and also prevent little things such as tea towels getting a larger deal they need to be.

4) making more time to your distant one on these

Your remote staff members cannot stop from the office easily catch you from the center of this day to ask a question or provide comments on a job. Additionally they cannot attend the workplace happy hour to construct relationship with you.

Plus, as we spoke about before, it's easy to misunderstand purpose when communication online.

The finest approach to cancel each one of these problems effectively would be to spend more time in one on people with your distant team members.

Longer one-on-one help you've got sufficient time to construct relationship with your remote workers. That attachment goes a ways towards helping counter the challenges we have previously covered now. Rapport makes communicating fitter, getting and providing feedback simpler, and it could even enhance participation.

But, the only method to build that connection with your remote workers, would be to commit time to make it. When you are on a phone, it can be quite simple to remain efficient and formal, remaining on task. Resist that temptation and then create some small talk. Ask how their loved ones is, be inquisitive about their vacations, and have an interest in getting to understand them.

This all begins with your own schedule. Establish an hour to the 1 on 1s together each week, and then allow there to be some little talk in different meetings. Perhaps it doesn't look like at the brief term it's a solid roi, but also the base is priceless. Additionally, it makes work more enjoyable and more interesting because you get to understand what makes different men and women tick.

5) whiteboarding and ideating with no at precisely the same conference room

Sharing notions between distant team members is obviously more challenging. That is mainly because you are missing that crucial workplace part of a frequent space.

Remote workers have nowhere they could proceed to riff on a thought that just popped into their mind. In the same way, remote workers miss those pesky discussions about alterations to merchandise, good thoughts, or even last-minute job changes.

If you've got remote employees in your staff, that fundamental area where you could go has to become electronic. This makes whiteboarding and ideating/brainstorming generally much harder.

Programs for whiteboarding and brainstorming with distant employees/teams

Frequently, distant teams will fly to meet every other especially for whiteboarding and profound, inventive, project cooperation. This will make the entire process a massive pain, and direct to crucial talks getting put off more than they ought to.

Fortunately. There are plenty of tools which make this process simpler.

6) spending more time handling and recording procedures

Placing up and handling procedures inside distant teams takes longer work—which includes partially distant teams, not simply those entirely distant.

Fast discussions in the workplace accumulate fast. Not only do queries get answered quicker this manner, many company culture standards become hauled by what is spoken, and also what individuals see others performing. Regrettably, remote workers only observe a tiny portion of these things, and that means you have to compensate for this.

This goes to a number of scenarios. Whether an unplanned conversation occurs just with those on your workplace, your distant employees are not engaged in the conversation, and oblivious of its own result. They shed two times, and are left out of the loop.

To combat this, install clear procedures upfront that direct team members without even slowing down them.

7) planning and budgeting to get routine face-to-face time with distant workers

The concept of working with remote workers can be enchanting: managing a worker whom you check in with occasionally, has their job done independently, and normally saves you on wages by being in a position to employ external expensive areas such as silicon valley.

The issue is, nothing surpasses the magic of face-to-face interaction to the two creative work and communicating. Simply because one of your workers is distant does not mean you don't ever need to meet in person.

Ideally, you ought to be flying distant workers in frequently, as far as each quarter based on preference and demand. Therefore, as you might be saving on wages, you ought to really be using some of the savings on flying folks out to match the remainder of the group.

8) praise and parties tend to be more difficult, and frequently unequal, for distant team members

It is simple to head out for drinks or even have a fast high-five at the workplace. Some companies even ring a bell or hit a gong for large wins or bargains shut. With distant team members, easy acts of celebration and praise are harder, since they overlook those items.

One on people are always a wonderful spot to provide compliments and congratulate them but set events are almost impossible to arrange exactly the exact same manner that you can to get a neighborhood team member.

The last thing you need is to get one of your distant team members to feel drained and they are not valued the exact same manner other staff members really are. Luckily, there are a number of things you can do in order to enhance this.

9) your distant workers may experience acute loneliness

Feeling like you are from this loop, and below valued aren't the only challenges which distant workers confront.

Working remotely might seem like heaven: the capability to operate if you want, the liberty to have a break if you want it, reside where you prefer, and constantly dress comfortably. These are great perks, however the liberty you get working generously comes with a significant potential downside: isolation.

How stress is born (and why it matters)

The challenge for remote workers is they don't generally find enough chances to work out their own vagus nerve. Because of this, it gets out of shape and may even atrophy like every muscle in the human body.

How it's possible to assist in preventing solitude

As a supervisor, you have to be mindful of the consequences of isolation on distant team members. It is not up for you, however you will find things you can do in order to promote those working below you to participate socially with the group.

First and foremost, you ought to chat about where your distant employee intends to get the job done.

Instead, he states inviting distant workers to become shared office area (no more co-working, which he says could be overly distracting) has assisted with groups he has worked with.

10) taxes, regulations, regulations and other legal documents

Do your prospective or current distant employees operate in precisely the exact same state? Exactly the identical state even? If you are in california, and also you employ somebody in florida, do you really know what sort of tax and other logistical paperwork you will want to look after?

Hiring individuals in various countries are going to have many distinct principles, and as a result of that many managers and founders tend to be on top of this. But just as significant can usually be hiring across country lines.

Each state might have different regulations and rules to follow along with taxation to document. You also must cover items such as unemployment insurance, and worker's settlement, individually for each nation.

The hidden costs of employing distant

What was differently a few quick entrances on your payroll system may easily receive a whole lot more complex and time consuming since you are hiring distant employees.

Most important is not to forget that government regulations and rules are severe; you cannot clarify away issues, nor"request forgiveness rather than consent" as it comes to these items. You'll get caught, and you'll receive fines.

Therefore, as soon as it's fascinating to include new hires out of a brand new region, you will need to be certain to place in the suitable time and consult with the right aid in remaining compliant in each and every nation and say to pay your bases and funding for any additional costs.

The very best way to keep in front of the is to perform the next:

1. Before hiring somebody at a new country or nation, speak with hr and lawful to be certain that there aren't any specific considerations to bear in mind.

2. Speak to your payroll supplier to learn what they are able to automate for you personally and what they advocate. Even for items they cannot do so, they frequently could point you into the ideal authorities site.

3. Consult your prospective new distant worker, since they might have gone through each the very same decoration in a prior job.

Being a supervisor isn't always glamorous. This is a good illustration of unsexy, nevertheless required function, to make sure your next distant hire comes on board easily, along with your organization avoids any unanticipated fines or offenses.

11) not everyone is a match for distant, even when they state they're

Earlier, we spoke about a few of their most frequent challenges for remote employees. Among the most frequently mentioned was using the subject to turn away:

Discipline plays a job on the reverse side too: you want to be intelligent enough to sit down every morning and get work done with no (or hardly any) outside reinforcement. Remote employees have a lot of liberty, but an equivalent quantity of responsibility includes this too.

Perhaps not everybody has the subject or customs to get this done. A lot of men and women benefit a lot from using a commute into work, sitting around their peers, then leaving when everybody else can. There is not anything wrong with having that ecological arrangement, but this usually means that person might not be a fantastic remote worker, even when they believed they could manage it.

How to discover if somebody is successful working remotely

As a supervisor, it is hard to understand if a person is a match for distant work prior to employing them.

But, once hired, you have to balance themhaving them fail to provide for a long time. As we have discussed earlier on the site, you can use the idea of task relevant maturity together:

Start out checking more often, and provide them smaller jobs you know could be delivered immediately. As they reach landmarks and build momentum, then they will have much more confidence, so will you. You may then back and be certain they can manage remote function, or even be hands on to help them construct the ideal distant habits or proceed in the occupation.

Expertise = the single effective evaluation of self-discipline

The very best approach to guarantee somebody can perform remote work nicely at your business would be to employ somebody who has done it all before. Afterward they could speak especially to the way they've made it work previously throughout the interview procedure.

Luckily, with the growth of not only full time distant function, but a lot of companies embracing work at home days, a lot more people are becoming expertise working remotely than you might anticipate.

Even better, those distant veterans are frequently more experienced workers too. Stack overflow's yearly survey of 90,000 programmers found,"developers who operate remotely fulltime have on average approximately 60 percent more years of specialist coding experience than people who do."

This suggests workers need more expertise in their livelihood before they are all set to efficiently operate distant. If a possible hire does not yet have a lot of expertise in their discipline, however gifted, they are much less likely to possess the subject or expertise required to operate remotely.

This also makes sense if you take into consideration the challenges of mentorship and training. When there are resources emerging attempting to create things such as pair programming simpler remotely, it is a lot simpler to coach somebody in person because it stands now.

To prevent running into problems of individuals failing to get the area to operate remotely, and consider focusing your distant work hires about the functions requiring additional expertise. And if that is not feasible, be ready to track new distant workers a little more carefully since they begin to guarantee they're starting off on the ideal foot with your staff.

12) all distant or none distant is a lot easier than a distant

There is a difference between entirely dispersed teams and teams which have a couple distant workers.

With fully dispersed teams, distant is the standard. There's not any feeling left from parties, not being hunted around for promotions or new duties, and everybody understands what it is like working distant.

But, using a combined group, or one in which you simply have just a few distant employees, the scenario changes completely.

With mixed teams where many, or most, of this group functions on-location, distant team members frequently overlook. They overlook last-minute meetings, end-of-the-week joyful moments, and all types of other crucial interactions that you get at the workplace.

Team members also might not have educated the instincts and habits to consider coworkers they do not see at work every day. Being made out and from this loop becomes the standard for distant workers especially in such scenarios.

The struggles of handling partially distant teams

We have already touched on a number of the matters remote workers overlook, but it is important that you understand that lots of those battles just apply to partly distant groups. Completely remote teams tend to be better in fixing the above challenges, since they have to; yet nothing else could get done differently, and they believe with respect to remote first.

As you seem to include distant hires for your organization, or devote all of the way into a fully distant company, it is crucial that you do this with open eyes. That is for the interest and also for those possible hires. Especially think about the numerous implications and changes which have to happen to help hiring your very first remote worker in the event the remaining part of the group is on-location.

Chapter three

The complete guide to grow your company on the web.

How internet marketing can help boost your small business

As more customers and business buyers venture on line (around 80 percent of shoppers study their next buy on line), organizations are beginning to explore how internet advertising can assist their company grow within another decade and past.

How will online advertising help your organization increase its earnings, earnings, and general growth?

Maintain reading this removable online advertising manual to learn. Learn about internet marketing, by what it would be to just how much it really costs, and receive the info that you want to convince company decision-makers into sign-on and maintain all of the benefits of electronic advertising.

If you're on the lookout for skilled online advertising aid, our award-winning group of over 200 internet strategists will help. Together with our custom plans, innovative artificial intelligence applications, and remarkable outcomes, we could create a solution which helps your company grow.

What is online marketing?

Online advertising, also referred to as internet advertising, clarifies the usage of online channels to market, promote, and promote a business and its manufacturer. Firms can leverage many different channels, such as email, search, social networking, and much more.

Just how is online advertising distinct from classic advertising?

Even though classic advertising and internet advertising help your company grow, they're distinct.

In comparison to conventional advertising, online advertising utilizes online channels. It occurs completely online. A conventional marketing and advertising strategy takes advantage of stations away from the world wide web, such as radio, print, and tv.

Channels are not the sole place where conventional and internet advertising disagree.

Price is another region of separation.

With online advertising, businesses of all sizes could get affordable possibilities for advertising and marketing their own enterprise, such as social networking marketing or search engine optimisation (search engine optimization). In contrast, traditional advertising tends to pose a high price that just name-brands can manage.

The affordability of internet advertising can often lead to a greater return on investment (roi) too.

Even though distinct, businesses are able to make the most of classic advertising and internet advertising. Collectively, an effort that frees both strategies can assist your company accelerate its development, earnings, and general exposure in the market.

5 advantages of online advertising (and how it can help your company)

Internet advertising assists your company in many ways, such as by supplying:

1. Measurable tactics to monitor the performance of various approaches and stations

2. Actionable information for enhancing the performance of plans, such as an advertising campaign

3. Cost-effective paths for earning sales and leads

4. Low price of entry for starting a plan or station

5. Insightful user information to improve advertising and targeting campaigns

In brief, online advertising offers your company a transparent socket for assessing and measuring the operation of your advertising and marketing strategies. And of course, it gives a flat and cheap playing area for the organization to compete with opponents.

What are a few online advertising strategies which may help my business?

A some of the most frequent online advertising approaches include:

Search engine optimization (search engine optimization)

Seo, or search engine optimisation refers to the way a site is optimized to do better at search results. Without seo, companies might find it hard to position on search engines such as google for the key words they connect with their services or products.

Optimizing your site for research is among the very best methods to cultivate your website traffic and your company.

Studies have discovered that being in the peak of the very first page of search results may make you more than 50 percent of visitors. But that percentage drops all of the way into a mere 4 percent to the fifth place. Thus, if you are not displaying on the very first page for a particular key word or phrase, then you'll forget about getting traffic like that!

To use seo to increase your company, you might choose to operate with an professional search engine optimization agency.

An seo company can help you execute the following jobs:

1. Assess your opponents

2. Describe the keywords and phrases you need to position for

3. Optimize your site names and meta tags

4. Boost your backup and search-engine content

5. Submit your website to search engines

6. With no seo, your company stands very little prospect of being discovered through searches.

Even though you may rank obviously for some key words with the years, actively optimizing your site is just one of the only techniques to conquer your competition and increase to the peak of the search outcome. It is among the most effective ways of any business to cultivate internet enterprise.

One of the top sections of seo is that it creates organic traffic that you are not paying after an initial investment. If you produce an wonderful blog article that begins ranking on very top of google for a specific search term, it is going to continue to attract in visitors day after day.

Seo permits for a potentially amazing yield on a relatively small initial investment.

That is why it is an exceptional illustration of how web advertising helps companies expand.

Pay-per-click (ppc) advertising

Ppc, or pay-per-click advertisements, is one other means to attract visitors to your site. Ppc advertisements are displayed along with search results and lure customers to click on these to get what they're searching for. As its name suggests, these advertisements ask that you pay every time a person clicks on your advertisement.

But, they are not as pricey as you may think.

In fact, the precise opposite is frequently correct. Ppc could be a wonderful investment for companies of all dimensions, as you've got intense control over your advertising spend. When competition is reduced, you might just pay a few pennies per click and see a fantastic return on investment.

Just such as seo, in which your ppc ads appear in search results are extremely important.

If your advertisement shows from the very first place, over the outstanding search results, your organization will receive approximately 59 percent of ad clicks. So it's crucial to invest in your ppc efforts to produce your enterprise link both observable and intriguing to shoppers.

Ppc campaign management could be a really complex and time-consuming procedure.

But, the outcomes are usually well worth it.

Ppc advertisements can induce a good deal of visitors, and might occasionally have an extremely large conversion rate if they're targeted toward particular search phrases.

For example, if you produce an advertisement for the term for"purchase crab cages," somebody who clicks it is likely seeking to do exactly that.

One growing type of ppc is facebook marketing.

Facebook advertisements could be highly targeted, and also will be able to assist you to increase not just your website visitors, but also drive brand new lovers to your fb business page. Several internet retailers find amazing results with advertisements on facebook, since it provides them the chance to immediately target their audience or market without spending a great deal of cash.

Social media marketing and advertising

Social media stations, such as facebook, twitter, and pinterest, are fantastic techniques for developing your company with internet advertising.

Firms can install official new pages or reports on social networking websites, and article updates to enthusiasts nevertheless often they select. While handling your existence on social media could possibly eat up a great deal of time especially if you're a really large manufacturer—it is well worth the investment.

Right from this gate, company owners must see that the intent of social networking is to be more sociable, to not only article promotional messages.

All these platforms provide enthusiasts of your organization or product brand new approaches to socialize, and find out about, exactly what you need to offer you. Additionally, it provides customers the chance to ask questions, seek help with some thing they're having difficulty with, or merely have a dialogue with you!

Social media helps grow your company by growing your buffs on these various platforms.

If someone follows on twitter since they enjoy what you need to state, they may finally make a buy from the site. Or, if a person joins your fb page as a friend recommended it, then they might expect you enough to sign up for a service once the timing is proper.

To place it simply, societal networking expansion = small business development.

There are a lot of innovative ways to use social networking to cultivate your fan and client base.

You may place links to interesting content (even if it is not your own!), run competitions or private promotions, or just ask questions. You're able to survey customers to their own view on new services or products, or request their comments on your site.

Above all else, it is vital to ensure fans know just how much you appreciate them. After all, where could you be with no clients?

In addition to marketing on interpersonal networking, you may even promote.

Whether your organization uses linkedin, facebook, twitter, pinterest, as well as snapchat, it is possible to start an advertising campaign. These campaigns tend to be highly concentrated, enabling you to achieve consumers through interests, behaviors, and much more.

If you would like to maximize the effects of the online advertising strategy, promote on social networking.

Email marketing

Email advertising is 1 way of developing your internet company that looks like it is going to continue forever.

Even though getting a dedicated following may have quite a very long time, manufacturers with big email lists are aware there is excellent value in this process. In reality, 1 study indicated that for every dollar a new spent in their email advertising plan, they created over $40!

Email's effectiveness appears to stem from its capacity to place your business directly where it matters most: a client's inbox. In this electronic age, the email address is among the most often accessed locations online. When a client opts-in to a own email list, they're saying they wish to provide your messages a property in their own inbox so you ought to definitely make the most of it!

By sending out regular emails about new products, specials or sales, and also intriguing additions to your site, it is possible to drive shoppers back to repeat purchases. Emails may also readily be forwarded to other people, so readers to a list may send you one of your advertising and marketing messages to your friend or relative should they see something of interest for them.

That can cause more subscriptions, more clicks, more and much additional earnings.

Email advertising is an established method to drive earnings and promote repeat traffic. You only have to take care to not overwhelm your readers! Brands should examine their email efficacy to find out the perfect time and frequency of the messages. Should you send too many mails, you risk irritating your clients—but not sufficient, and they could forget you entirely.

Content marketing

Content marketing denotes the plan of advertising to prospective clients with various kinds of content.

The content employed within this method may differ from websites for videos to whitepapers or perhaps ebooks, however all of them share exactly the identical end purpose: to convince visitors to a site they ought to purchase from or associate with you.

A strong content promoting technique can help you develop your small business on the internet in bounds and leaps. Believe it or not, clients love first content, and a number of studies have proven that brands offering original content are far more dependable than brands which don't.

One of the earliest methods of articles promotion is the business website.

A site may be a terrific way to not only provide content that's intriguing to people visiting your site, but also to make conversation and promote repeat visits. Websites do not need to worry about all on your products or brand; in actuality, the majority of business blogs have a tendency to concentrate on their business as a whole, researching ideas or tendencies and the way they relate to their own goods.

Content marketing may also arrive in the kind of downloadable, long-form articles, such as whitepapers, manuals, or ebooks.

Even though this type of articles can have quite a very long time to get a new to create and requires additional study and tools in relation to a simple blog article, it can be quite rewarding. Offering long-form articles can help position you as a consideration or business pioneer, and that sort of placement can be exceedingly valuable.

When implemented properly, content promotion will continue to keep your clients interested in your own brand. They'll be inclined to return and see your website frequently for new items to see and digest. If you are limited in time, then you always have the option to invest in content advertising services or perhaps copywriting solutions.

Outreach

Links, in addition to outreach, are different ways that prospective customers may discover your small business.

If someone is visiting a site they hope, and they visit that a url to your website, they're a lot more inclined to trust you when they could if they'd stumbled upon you at another method. However getting links on other sites is not about hope: it is also on your own ranking.

Links to your website help signify how well you need to position in searches for certain key words or phrases.

Search engine calculations—the way search engines determine by which a site ranks in natural outcomes—have evolved since their debut.

Years past, the site that had the maximum key words, the most hyperlinks, and also the keywords in their articles will sit in the #1 place. But, algorithms currently take supernatural or supernatural behavior under account. This usually means that it is not sufficient to have a great deal of connections—they need to be high quality hyperlinks from trusted and well-known websites.

So, to be able to find these fantastic links and enhance your rank, you'll have to undergo a procedure called link construction.

This describes the procedure for creating links to your website from different websites through manual activities. There are dozens and dozens of link building choices on the market! It is possible to just request a connection, or you'll be able to produce great content which others wish to connect to. Social networking and pr are two other methods which you can find these precious links.

If you're able to develop a great deal of high-quality hyperlinks to your organization online, this can imply to search engines and sellers they can trust you. This won't just enhance your rank, but also boost the quantity of traffic which comes to your website.

Responsive or mobile-friendly web design

Site traffic from mobile phones and tablet computers raises daily.

More and more customers are using their mobile devices to study, navigate, and also store on the move.

To grow your business on the internet, you might find it essential to make a mobile-optimized site or possibly an entirely mobile version of your website.

Mobile site design often entails installing specific code which can make your site a lot easier to browse a cell phone or tablet computer. It'll reduce unnecessary zooming or scrolling, and certainly will make it simpler for clients to get what they're searching for—or perhaps earn a buy—out of their apparatus.

Creating a cell version of your site, or utilizing reactive design to make sure your current content appears correctly on all apparatus, can possibly raise your conversion rate radically.

If a shopper visits your website in their telephone and finds it effortless to browse, they're a lot more inclined to purchase from you than in a company who doesn't have a mobile-friendly shop.

This online advertising approach helps your company hugely. Supplying your site traffic with a quick, easy-to-use site raises their odds of engaging with your business, such as by buying your merchandise or calling your staff.

5 suggestions to maximize the advantages of online marketing

Do you wish to update the advantages of internet marketing on your company? Try out these five suggestions:

Respond to internet testimonials: get together with your clients and company buyers. Whether individuals leave testimonials on google, facebook, or a different station, react to all those testimonials. Thank users due to their favorable comments and assist users who had a negative encounter.

Maintain nap info up-to-date: to the best effects with internet marketing, make sure that the name, address, and telephone number are true throughout stations. Including your site, social networking reports, and anyplace else where your telephone and location information seems.

Evaluation website features: construct an"constantly be analyzing" strategy, and you're able to enhance conversion speeds throughout your website. When you experimentation with different backup on an agency page or fresh designs, you may use information to make a better consumer experience.

Gain seo inspiration with ppc: businesses which use ppc can leverage effort data within their search engine optimization strategy. Via keyword data in the ppc campaign, you are able to find new key phrases to goal as part of your search engine optimization campaigns, which will be able to help you draw valuable visitors to your website.

Utilize video to increase communicating: a movie will help consumers of all backgrounds and experience levels know your small business. Whether you are attempting to describe exactly how a product works or a item assists, you may use a movie to describe the subject in a means which is logical for everyone.

How do I begin with web advertising?

If you are searching to utilize internet advertising to help your business grow, it is vital to construct a good foundation for the plan. Getting started with internet marketing may take some time with all these foundation-building measures, but they pay off at the long term.

Start your electronic marketing and advertising strategy together with the next measures:

Ascertain exactly what you wish to achieve with internet marketing, such as bringing in prospects or revenue

Research the stations open to your small business and the way they'd help attain those aims

Compile study on your intended market to narrow your listing of stations farther

Select the stations which align with your targets and give the best value

Establish a realistic budget to every station

Build your plan for each station, in addition to your general plan

Establish your aims and track their functionality

Quantify your results and create upgrades to increase functionality

With these measures, your company can construct a wise strategy for advertising and marketing your business across online channels. Whether you choose to utilize seo, ppc, or a different strategy, it is possible to grow your internet reach, earnings, and much more.

Get professional online marketing help for the enterprise

Internet marketing is evolving, constantly changing and never staying the same.

There are constantly new social networking stations to research, added modifications to google's algorithm, and also upgraded "best practices" for internet marketers. That means you could wonder how internet advertising can assist your company when nothing stays the same.

In this electronic era, you might discover that it's hard to keep up with the most recent internet advertising trends and just how much marketing and advertising prices. As a busy small business owner, you've to do and upgrading your site copy likely is not in your list of priorities.

That is why internet marketing firms such as webfx exist!

We will help you make sense of electronic advertising, and also get you to the ideal path to achievement. We've got the experience, know-how, and gifted team to provide internet advertising aid in every conceivable manner—and we would like to utilize it in order to grow your enterprise.

15 ideas to boost your company on the internet (without a great deal of cash)

Looking to develop your small business online without a great deal of cash? If you're just starting a company, then you can't afford to squander money. Within the following guide, we'll discuss practical suggestions about the best way best to raise your company on a budget. Our intention is to assist you compete with the big men without having to spend a lot of money.

1. Select the ideal platform to your site

The biggest mistake you may earn as a small company is picking the wrong stage to construct your site. A incorrect platform are not only going to cost you more cash, but additionally, it will restrict your business' expansion possible.

We advocate using wordpress. It's by far the most popular site builder on the current market, and it forces over 31 percent of websites (such as both small and massive companies).

When we state wordpress, we're speaking about wordpress.org rather than wordpress.com. They're two distinct platforms, visit our post about the gap between wordpress.com vs wordpress.org for additional information.

To begin a self-hosted wordpress site, you are going to require a domain name and a web hosting accounts. Yes, they are different. Want to discover more? Watch our explanation: what is the difference between domain vs internet hosting.

Different hosting companies offer various plans acceptable for small to large sites. This ultimately impacts the price of your site.

If you're only starting out, then we advocate using bluehost. They're among the biggest hosting companies on the planet and also an officially advocated wordpress hosting supplier.

Fortunately, they're offering wpbeginner customers totally free domain name and reduction hosting. Essentially, you are going to have the ability to get started for about $ 2.75 a month.

2. Opt for a functional site with simple layout

Many beginners feel that their clients won't take their business seriously if they don't possess their site professionally equipped.

Obtaining an expert to custom designing your site is pricey, and it is not required when you are just beginning.

You can easily begin with a readymade premium or free wordpress motif for a portion of a cost.

Watch our expert's choice of the ideal wordpress topics to get some inspiration.

1. Finest wordpress firm topics

2. Finest woocommerce wordpress topics

3. Finest free wordpress topics

If not one of the aforementioned themes suit your own need, then you might also utilize these drag & drop wordpress site builders to produce fully custom layouts without writing any code.

3. Make it easier for consumers to get you

If you would like your site to attract more clients, then you want to bring a simple way for people to get in touch with you.

The simplest way to do this is using a contact form in your site.

By default, wordpress does not arrive with a contact type. Fortunately, are wordpress contact type plugins which could assist you easily incorporate a contact form to your website.

We advocate using wpforms lite. It's the free version of the favorite wpforms plugin that is trusted by more than 1 million sites.

After your company has increased, it is possible to update to wpforms guru to make more innovative forms like polls, surveys, payment types, etc..

4. Start building an email list out of day 1

Most individuals who abandon your site won't ever return again. This usually means that in case you do not obtain their email address, then you'll not have a way to speak together later on.

The most cost-effective means to do so is by creating an email list.

Email promotion has become the most dependable method to convey with your site traffic.

You can begin with continuous contact, they are the best rated email advertising service supplier in our listing.

Wpbeginner users receive a free trial for people who're just beginning and 20 percent off, should you update to their paid program.

For more hints, visit our newcomer's guide on how best to perform direct generation in wordpress just like an expert.

5. Get more organic traffic from search engines

Search engines such as google would be the significant source of visitors for the majority of sites online. There are a whole lot of things you can do in order to optimize your site to search engines by studying basic seo.

Seo or search engine optimisation is really a set of tips and techniques which produce your site search engine friendly. It's never overly specialized and you'll have the ability to get it done all on your own.

We have printed a whole step by step wordpress seo manual for novices. We'll help you through the full procedure for producing your site as seo friendly as possible.

To get visitors from search engines you are going to want articles, which brings us into another step within this guide.

6. Plan a content advertising strategy

Content advertising is a way to make useful and appropriate content to pull and build up an audience. This permits you to gain more targetted visitors from search engines without spending a lot of money.

The simplest way to add valuable content to your site is by simply including a blog. Wordpress permits you to bring another site page to your site and type your articles into groups and tags.

You have to plan your own content plan by figuring out the key words your users could possibly be on the lookout for. View our guide on how to perform keyword search for your own blog.

Want thoughts about the best way best to use those key words in your content strategy? Here's a huge collection of blog article tips which you could use on your own site.

Content advertising is an extremely successful and proven approach to advertise your company on a budget. To find out more about it, then see this manual about the best way best to make a productive content advertising plan for your company.

7. Create data-based choices with google analytics

Many beginners utilize their best guesses to program their own expansion plan. You do not have to do this when you're able to use real data to make those choices.

This is where google analytics is sold in. It permits you to see just how many people have been coming to your website, where they're coming from, and also exactly what they do while.

Watch our guide about the best way best to set up google analytics from wordpress for step by step directions.

Google analytics includes a great deal of info. Though it's neatly arranged and superbly presented, it might still be somewhat overwhelming for users.

To get the absolute most from it, set up and activate the monsterinsights plugin. It's the finest google analytics plugin for wordpress also permits you to easily see your main traffic reports within wordpress dashboard. If you operate an internet shop, then monsterinsights may also allow you to monitor woocommerce clients utilizing google analytics.

You may also obtain the free version of monsterinsights. It works good but you would not have access to a number of its advanced capabilities.

8. Leverage social media to drive traffic

Social media programs have tremendously engaged crowds. Facebook alone has 1.47 billion daily busy users, that is around 18 percent of people on the planet. Twitter, youtube, linkedin, along with other societal networking platforms have users that are highly engaged.

With numerous consumers, social networking platforms deliver great opportunities for company. You may begin with making your company's social networking profiles and mechanically sharing your own blog articles.

Next, you'd wish to make it a lot easier for your customers to discuss your articles on social networking. For that you'll require a social networking plugin for wordpress. These plugins include societal sharing buttons for a wordpress website.

There are plenty of different things which you may do in order to engage with viewers on social networking. The crucial thing is to maintain your profiles busy, grow your next, and bring visitors back to your site.

1. Produce a facebook group to your clients or business

2. Produce a linkedin set for your business

3. Discover to retarget consumers on facebook with advertisements

4. Concentrate on interpersonal networks essential to your own industry. By way of instance, if you operate a style site or restaurant you might find instagram more useful than linkedin.

5. Do not simply bring traffic to your site, use social networking to construct your email list

9. Make an active player in online communities

Online communities contain forums and question-answer sites. All these are the places people go to place their queries, socialize, locate articles, and research. Leading communities online comprise reddit, stack exchange, quora, tripadvisor, and much more.

All these communities supply you with access to individuals interested in subjects connected with your business. It's possible to combine them at no cost and spend time in developing ability.

First, you have to learn which communities are more applicable to your enterprise and where your potential clients may go searching for content or answers. By way of instance, if you operate a travel site, you might find tripadvisor more useful than other divisions.

Do not spam those forums with links to your site in every post. Build authority by truly engaging with useful articles, and mention your organization or site when it's suitable.

10. Merge abandoning website visitors into customers

Did you understand that over 70 percent of individuals that see your site won't ever find it ? It's not your fault, but it is just that the world wide web is really large and there are many sites out there.

Each visitor that leaves your site is a prospective client that you're losing. To increase your company, you have to concentrate on converting people into paying clients.

This is where optinmonster is sold from. It's the ideal conversion optimization program on the current market, which permits you to convert casual site visitors into loyal clients.

Just how does it do this?

It has a drag and fall effort builder where you are able to produce various kinds of efforts to accumulate user mails, exhibit special offerings, reveal exit-intent popups, countdown timers, intelligent popups, slide-in optins, and much more.

11. Begin an affiliate partner program

Affiliate advertising is a referral agreement where an internet merchant (advertiser) pays commission into some referrer if users buy a product with their referral link.

If you sell goods on the internet, then you are able to use affiliate marketing to associate with proficient affiliate marketers. You'll pay a sales commission to such entrepreneurs for boosting your goods and bringing you revenue.

You will require an affiliate management platform to monitor referral action and payout your own affiliate associates. This is our listing of top affiliate management and monitoring software which you are able to utilize.

You may also encourage other people's services or products to create additional cash from the own content. Watch our internet affiliate advertising guide for tools and tips you will want to begin.

12. Use pay-per-click advertising

Unlike to popular beliefthat it is possible to conduct pay-per-click marketing campaigns on a little budget. With programs such as google adwords and facebook advertising, you may put your own pricing, target keywords, viewers, and much more.

In reality, google adwords also has free advertisement credits for new advertisers. Bluehost, a reliable wordpress hosting firm also supplies complimentary google adwords credits using their hosting plans.

You can make use of these credits to experimentation with ppc advertisements and find some paid visitors to your site at no cost.

13. Utilize social proof to acquire customers

Social evidence is a mental phenomenon where individuals conform to the activities of the others under the premise that those activities are reflective of the suitable behaviour.

Marketers utilize this happening by demonstrating their clients which other individuals already trust a solution or company. This is carried out by sharing their data, or subscriber points, client testimonials, and much more.

Here is an inventory of smart tactics to use social evidence on your site to boost conversions.

14. Effectively utilize fomo to boost revenue and conversions

Fomo or'anxiety about missing ' is an emotional term used to refer to stress about overlooking some thing fascinating and fashionable.

As a company, you are able to make the most of the human behaviour and use it in order to improve conversions and sales. Essentially, you have to construct anxiety with the addition of scarcity to your supplies. Here's an excellent illustration from booking.com using lack to construct anxiety.

15. Boost your site's rate and performance

Studies show from 2000 to 2016, the average human attention span has fallen from 12 minutes to 7 minutes.

As a website proprietor, this usually means you've hardly any time to show consumers everything you've got to give and convince them to remain on your site.

Another study discovered that a 1 minute delay in page loading time may result in a 7 percent reduction in conversions, 11 percent fewer page views, and also a 16 percent reduction in consumer satisfaction.

This means that you will need to optimize your site to ensure it is quickly and works nicely under high traffic.

Follow the directions in our step-by-step guide to enhance wordpress rate and functionality for novices. This guide contains all of the tips that we use on our really large traffic sites for dependable speed and functionality.

We expect that this article helped you understand how to raise your company on a shoestring budget. You might also need to see that our specialist selection of the very helpful tools to handle and develop your site.

Chapter four

15 important actions to starting and growing your own online business

There is no doubt that we're living in interesting financial times. And we've got the alternative of concealing and withdrawing away from these be courageous, get creative and think of successful solutions to be left behind.

There is a developing set of ordinary people whom I prefer to call"time and money experts" that chose to take things in their own hands and develop strategies to make additional cash to escape debt sooner, save for emergencies and also bring a minumum of one parent house to ensure that both did not need to be off in their various tasks while somebody else infant sat their kids.

Sure, perhaps it doesn't simple to do and it requires a little work, however it's straightforward, and there is a huge difference.

Here are 15 measures many of these took as a way to win against the market and make more cash in their spare moment, then part time and finally fulltime.

Measure 1:

They understood that anything they were doing for a long time wasn't functioning in addition to they expected it would and made a choice to locate different solutions.

Measure 2:

They made a listing of all of the things they like doing and are proficient at.

For example, things such as for example gardening, hiking, sowing, designing sites, playing a musical instrument, remaining healthy and healthy, producing clothes or hair accessories.

Measure 3:

They then did a little investigating to discover whether or not there is a need for information, services or products in their own fields of interest and ability.

One method to do this is by using the free"keyword tool - google adwords" and comparing distinct variant of these phrases and words a user could utilize in a google search to locate these goods, services or advice.

For example, example:"the best way to develop a garden in warm weather" would create a particular number of searches that have been performed each month by consumers all around the world.

A amount that's too large would signal a great deal of competition. Too low may indicate a tiny sector.

This isn't to say that you should or shouldn't get in that marketplace based on that data alone, but it's a great place to get started.

Subsequently it is an issue of looking at some other sources of advice to find out whether cash can be reached in a particular section.

For case in point:

1. Are there any celebrities which are geared on this marketplace? If this is so, it's very likely that there's cash to be left there. Why would publishers squander their resources and money to set out a magazine which nobody will purchase or sign up to? Right?

2. Are there some bestselling novels on the topic?

3. What is the"buzz" offline and online about it?

4. It will not take much to ascertain a marketplace with a solid need.

Measure 4:

Now it is time to find the contest. Who are you? Where are they all? How can they provide? What are clients saying about these? How can they sell? For how much? Just how long have they been in operation? How can they advertise? What makes them stand apart from one another?

After finding answers to other questions that you believe are significant, then it is time to research and think of a strategy to distinguish yourself from them in case you should enter company within that market.

What you do n't necessarily need to be"greater", even though that will benefit tremendously, but it ought to be"distinct" so it will entice a section of prospects your competition isn't catering to.

How will you shine and stick out from everybody else?

Measure 5:

After you choose your niche, be certain there are individuals eagerly looking for answers to problems you'll be able to help them are prepared and ready to pay you good money for your goods, services or advice, and are comparatively simple to accomplish through cheap mediums.

Measure 6:

Brainstorm what it is that you're likely to supply them, how you'll pack it and what you'll charge for this.

Measure 7:

Purchase a domain through businesses like 1and1. Com, for instance. At least that is where I buy minebut you ought to do your research to discover a business that you expect and provides you excellent value and assistance.

Measure 8:

Establish up a hosting accounts. I use a business named hostgator, however you can find several other respectable firms out there which you could perform research on.

Measure 9:

Establish your site or blog to capture your prospects' attention, create interest in your services and products, create want to them, and request them to do it (subscribe to a subscription to your paid or free newsletter, and buy your merchandise, employ your own services, etc.).

That is the classic"aida formula", incidentally. It is"care","interest","want" and"action."

Measure 10:

Start advertising and advertising your own site using either compensated methods and/or totally free ones, based upon your financial plan.

Those approaches include"pay per click" or"ppc" advertisements through search engines such as google, yahoo!, bing, etc., and facebook ppc; you can leasing a database or listing of readers on your market belonging to additional entrepreneurs or networks; and utilizing social networking websites like facebook, youtube, linkedin, twitter, squidoo, etc..

You can also locate other recognized site owners offering non-competing products to exactly the exact same niche market you're targeting and then request them to associate with you by boosting your goods or service for their own subscribers or clients in exchange for a proportion of their earnings.

Of but there are lots of other marketing and advertising procedures, but these are a fantastic location for you to begin.

Consistently bear in mind to compose your advertising and marketing pieces from the point of view of your client. Remember they're constantly asking:"what is in it for me?"

Make certain to answer that issue to their own satisfaction.

It isn't about you! It is all about what they need and what they're searching for.

Utilizing what is called"seller chat" is a surefire method to turn off prospects. Inform them your service or product is"the very best and best since the start of period" will surely have the absolute opposite effect of what you actually want.

It is far better inform them not just about the qualities of your service or product, but also its benefits and benefits, that can be more significant.

The aida formula may be effectively utilized in all of your marketing and promotion messages.

Measure 11:

After you begin getting traffic to your site, focus on analyzing various offers, headlines, images, etc. To be certain you convert as many visitors into readers and/or clients as you can.

Recall to test 1 component at a time so you can easily determine that change was accountable for your precise outcomes.

Measure 12:

Consistently offer your clients or customers the red carpet treatment. Be truthful with them. Treat them with respect. Listen to your own questions, doubts, suggestions and concerns. Ask them how you can better your services and products. Constantly under promise and over deliver.

Measure 13:

This is optional, but should you would like to grow, you ought to find some help. Perhaps this measure can be put before in the listing, but I believe that it's vital that you first understand as much as you can about your company before you begin outsourcing certain jobs to independent contractors or hire workers.

Just be sure to do comprehensive research on the folks that you'd love to bring to a group. Make certain they're"superstars" until you provide them a position in your company.

"be slow to employ, fast to fire" is the doctrine of several successful entrepreneurs. You do not need to agree with this, however it is a fantastic idea to consider what that doctrine could mean to your company.

Measure 14:

Be sure to guard your company through all the crucial methods, legal and otherwise.

Consult licensed professionals in the fields of business structures, bookkeeping, net safety, copyrightsand patents (if needed), insurance, etc..)

Measure 15:

Consistently bear in mind this, at least in my own estimation, it is best for you to have the company rather than that the company owns you.

Never lose sight of why you began the company in the first location. Could it be to offer your loved ones with a much better lifestyle? I am uncertain how much better it's going to be if you are not around much as your organization is taking almost all of your time.

I truly think that it is ideal to see a company as a way to an end, rather than the end result.

Do not fall in the trap that lots of entrepreneurs have dropped into by enabling their companies to become their own life rather than having a much better life due to their companies.

Of course there are several more important approaches and methods you should really know more about and also consider to raise the odds of getting successful and never be another casualty of about the path to entrepreneurship, however you realize that space is limited.

But, there's a comprehensive manual that covers exactly what I shared with you, and much more, in detail. It is called:"the time and money experts"

I wish you good success and remember never to stop since you will never know how near you are to the success you're searching for.

Salvador posada is a down-to-earth man who eventually came to know the wisdom from the phrases, so"follow the passion, not your own retirement" and"discover your passion and the money will follow" he possesses a couple of online companies and provides instruction, training and training to people who wish to make more income online doing exactly what they enjoy.

The way to begin creating your business's online

presence - topic 5

You might have owned your business for several decades, or are only starting the trip. Regardless, you're extremely aware the world wide web is generating wealth just like never before. But you do not have any idea how to promote yourself on the internet, nor do you really know where to start. Never stress, below are a few basic principles.

Measure 1: blogging, email/ezine marketing, and ebooking.

Just imagine. About 10-15 decades back, not one of those words occur, nevertheless, they've come to be some of the most crucial phrases in the current world to direct you towards your own route to success. You no longer could succeed by cold-calling. Today's successful small business owners compose"value messages" for their clientele. These worth messages include things which can help people, or build value in their own lives, but will stay directly associated with your small business.

Great suggestions for ezine posts. Listed below are a couple of"teach hints" to receive your staff to another level...

Educate everyone that mindset is the basis of success, both private and company

Educate everyone the value of friendliness

Educate everyone that rate of reaction is not an alternative

Educate everyone the best way to respond to customer complaints

Educate everyone that support is as significant as earnings

Educate everyone to request more company

Educate everyone to indicate more

Educate everyone to thank the client for their company

Additional matters to write about: listed below are some ideas that you may utilize to compose value messages for your clients. Please, don't hesitate to use or change them in any manner you see fit.

1. Just how and why you chose to begin your company"x" years back.

2. The battles you went through at the beginning phases.

3. The achievement you experienced through recent years.

4. The way you originally obtained customers.

5. Everything you did to help keep the customers coming backagain.

6. Just how much time it took you to become lucrative.

7. What you'd do different if you'd like to do it all around.

8. Why brand new and present clients choose you over the competition.

9. What's unique about your goods and/or assistance.

10. Your short term and longterm objectives.

11. The way you could enable a company owner build their company by buying your service or product.

Measure 2: dealing with other businesses

After you re-program your brain to concentrate on helping others, you will shortly start to see that the benefits come back.

The search engines position your website/business depending off the relativity and high quality of content, as well as the recognition of your webpage. Your main purpose is to reach the peak of the search engine every time a possible customer/client is looking for advice. The higher your rank, the more visitors that your website is going to get.

One fantastic means to do so is to search for businesses that you can associate with to send every other referrals. By way of instance, if you have a printing firm, discover another company who might refer business to you and vice versa.

I'm advocating you to contact and build partnerships with these kinds of firms in the sectors closely linked to your enterprise. As soon as you've assembled the relationships/partnerships, provide to set a hyperlink to their site on yours and after it is finished, request the exact same in return.

Measure 3: never quit studying

The second you stop improving yourself or expanding your company is going to be the instant your organization starts to decrease in succeeding. It might take ten or five decades, but finally the contest will transcend you. Do not ever find comfy. Do not ever get articles. Company b is working as hard, or even harder than you personally, to become company a.

Measure 4: utilizing the resources available

There are lots of excellent solutions available to assist you build your internet presence in little if any price. Each of these resources are critical to a success please, be certain that you make an account for every one of these.

Do not forget to place all of the accounts on your organization name. This is essential to maximize your internet presence. Nobody will understand who you are unless you tell them.

Due to editorial guidelines, we're likely to record the reports forms based off the popular search engines along with other societal and media websites on the market: email, business solutions, website analytics, website pay-per-click for search engine optimization, blogs, social media, forums, video upload sites, along with some other relevant website on the market.

I'm the proprietor and senior marketing analyst of suited marketing. I'm an entrepreneur and a visionary and a mentor and bonus. I am going to teach you how you can construct your very own successful enterprise. My 1st novel, money does grow on trees, is a motivational and inspirational novel and also my 2nd book, how money grows on tress, educates the nuts and bolts of how to raise your company along side-by-side training program.

My weekly ezine was made to take scenarios that you deal with on a daily basis and then link them to business in addition to enhancing your lifetime.

I look forward to working together and with you provide comments in my ebooks, site, training application, etc.. Please tell us how we're doing.

10 easy advertising tips to boost your company

There are hundreds of approaches to advertise and promote your own internet business. Ideally, you need to use quite a few of these on your promotional campaigns. Relying on just 1 approach is really a recipe for failure. Forums are among those lesser-used marketing and advertising methods, but it may be one of the most successful if utilized correctly.

There is a particular method to begin advertising with forums however. A lot of men and women believe that their earnings increase by incorporating more and more self-promotional substance. In fact, continuous self-promotion has the contrary effect. Folks might steer clear and you might be banned from this discussion. Prior to joining a discussion, it's quite important to browse through their principles and regulations.

To benefit out of forums, you will need to give in addition to take. Answer queries in your subject of expertise frequently. As a result, folks will come to view you as an authority within the specialty. As individuals read your articles and see which you're extremely educated, you will start to see an increasing number of forum members seeing your website.

If you wish to raise traffic or sales, you have to combine as many forums as you can, and require a while to read and reply articles. Start looking for queries or issues that are linked to your area of experience. If it is possible to answer these queries, you'll be seen of as an authority in your area or market. Everybody is on the lookout for help on particular topics. By helping other people, you will in fact be supporting yourself.

Forums are a terrific source for:

1. Boost your item. Input the url of your site or page on your signature (sig) file) every time you enter into a place to answer or ask a query, be certain that you include your sig file.

Do you wish to find out more about the way I make money? I've just finished my brand-new guide about the best way best to generate money every day.

2. Discover products to market. The forums have been full of individuals that are promoting goods. Look through the several articles to discover products that match your specialty.

3. Locate a profitable market to come up with products for. Assess article topics which have numerous queries. Normally, these are subjects people want to know more about. Pay attention to the forms of questions asked and the range of individuals asking identical questions. This will alert you to the demand for a specific item. Be certain that you experience these articles completely. In case the issue is full of individuals answering a query, it's not a candidate to receive your own ebook. In case the subject is composed mostly of queries, you might have found a lucrative market.

4. Get your site or sales page assessed. Many forums supply areas where it is possible to ask participants to reassess your own website. You ought to be conscious that you may sometimes become scathing reviews, so use this procedure only in the event that you're able to accept criticism.

5. Boost the page ranking of your site. Posting in forums, particularly well rated ones, can offer the website that you put on your sig file with links that are back. The search engines may view this advice and benefit your website accordingly.

6. Greater visitors to your site. I check my visitors frequently and that I see consistent visitors to my websites from forums that I post to. This is an established process to boost visitors.

7. Get advice on a commodity, service, or business prior to making a buy. A lot of men and women are more than pleased to provide you with their view on goods or businesses which they are knowledgeable about.

8. Create contacts. In the physical world, business card swaps abound. Forums can supply a similar purpose. They offer you the chance to develop business contacts without even leaving your house.

9. On the lookout for somebody to make a joint venture or any other mutually beneficial business bargain. Forums are filled with individuals that are receptive to joint ventures. You merely need to have on the market, make observations, and also article when proper.

10. Find a mentor. A lot of men and women would aid people who have less expertise at no cost. I've seen a number of articles offering to assist beginners.

Forums can be quite helpful to the seasoned marketer in addition to the newcomer. The most helpful forums are those connected to your website or niche. Look for those associated forums and your company will certainly benefit.

Chapter five
Online working

Actual online function

If you've been trying to earn an excess revenue on the internet, you would realize that actual online work is hard to locate these days on account of the number of scams all around the internet, nowadays it is tough to understand what's real and what's legit allow me to give you a couple of choices that might assist you in making some cash online.

Selecting the way you wish to earn money online is dependent on what you believe genuine online work, you will of heard folks make a neat little amount by filling out online surveys that is a simple small $3 job based on the number of polls you perform, however to be fair you want to be satisfying at least 70 polls per day to produce some significant cash, but still this legit way to make some money on the internet.

Another alternative is affiliate advertising, affiliate advertising is what I believe myself as actual on line work, why you ask, just because there's not any limit on which you are able to earn. But be cautioned, now there are many so called gurus available on the web who assert a new class they've developed is the actual bargain on earning some genuine hard money, you might have seen a few for instance, the way I made $300,000 in under 3 times. These kind of class are published every week around the and most men and women who need to generate some cash online wind up purchasing them and squandering there hard earned money on these products

Myself, i've been on the lookout for actual online work for quite a while now but just last month a buddy of mine introduce me into a internet advertising and marketing university, I was somewhat cautious, yes I confess i've attracted these so called ace ace goods that will assist you get x amount in below x number of months I took the lure and parted with my cash, but something was different about this internet school, it had been a place were that they provided each of the tools I wanted (which from how you may need to buy separately in the so called ace course which allowed them to make more income you off) but the something which struck me was the owners kyle and carson, are available to provide anybody 1on1 service whenever they wanted it. Something that's not provided at any online affiliate advertising universities, great i'd actually found something which will be actual online work which would create an income for me on line:d

So I united and allow me to tell you for about $97 per month, this had been the very best investment i've made up to now in my entire life, the college provides you many resources and training which it all combined needs to come to about $1600 per month, however they provide this also 1on1 coaching for $97 per month!! And its giving me actual online work because and allowed me to make an income on the internet and let me escape in the chains of a 9-5 job, also let me devote time with my loved ones.

However, I can't stress that enough, overall affiliate marketing isn't a get rich immediately strategy, but there is nothing as actual online work at which you are able to make x level by sitting doing something which appears to good to be true, however so long as you utilizes the techniques displayed in the college, you'll be on you way to earning an income online but even when you're stuck be certain to see the forum within the college and request assistance, I recommend also checking out the stories indoors these stories will provide you inspiration to be successful.

Online work opportunity

The www (world wide web) was spreading its tentacles, and it's due to that online job opportunities for gifted individuals have grown to a fantastic extent. Freelancing on the world wide web is now comfortable and simple for those that are curious and have some skill. Therefore, if you're only sitting idle and possess a great deal of time on your hands, think about some of those online work opportunities and begin working from your property. Whats more you get a fantastic cover for your job. We could also say the three'w's stand for:

· wherever you would like to get the job done!

· at any time you would like to get the job done!

· anything you would like to get the job done!

Thank you to the net now you can correct the job depending on your own life instead of doing the reverse. The attractiveness of working on the internet is that you don't have to be on the payroll of almost any 1 business. You may also opt to execute a lot of different functions at precisely the exact same time in accordance with your abilities. You do not have to be exceptionally competent to operate on the internet. A computer literate with a fantastic monitor and a secure online connection in your home, can certainly execute the jobs these work opportunities need.

You will first must pick from the a variety of online work opportunities also it's quite imperative that you select something you're interested in and therefore are capable of. Don't opt for something solely for the interest of cash, particularly if you're considering doing this on a long-term foundation.

You will discover various online functions in areas like transcriptionand medical transcription, technician support, client service, virtual assistant service, site design, content writing, proofreading, etc.. You have to choose wisely, select a job that's compatible with your abilities, nature and comfort tag. So you can continue it for quite a while and get the absolute most from it.

Everybody is well conscious of the simple fact that the world wide web is full of scams so there'll be tens of thousands who will attempt to rip off you. These scam artists provide you quite attractive job opportunities and once you turn into their support providerthey can bill you for many different fake motives and may not pay you after the agency is supplied. Try and steer clear of these types of offers since they're entirely scams. But do not hesitate, there are many other online work opportunities that can benefit you using a fantastic cover to the hard work.

Online work qualifications - five reasons why you need to use them

All companies have a couple of items in common, among these is for those who have employees you want to program these workers. Typical problems with relying on newspaper programs are; supervisors must physically be in the company to place the program, workers will need to phone in to be aware when they're functioning, and it's not time or cost effective. Below is a listing of just how using online programs can solve those problems together with other folks.

1. Managers may post programs from anywhere they have web.

As a supervisor, with work schedules on the internet you have the capacity to post up the schedule if you cannot get in the office on such day. Should you rely on writing or registering the program and print out it you must be in your company to place the program. By getting your schedules on line you can produce and place the programs by the comfort of your home.

2. Employees do not need to call.

When you own a schedule in the company your workers need to call to discover if they're working. Not only can it be inconvenient to them, but it's also inefficient. It disturbs your other workers throughout their work day whenever they must respond fellow workers calling to discover if they're working. This produce less distractions for workers functioning and also the benefit for workers that are looking to test when they're working in their moment. By employing online work programs, workers have access to this whenever they want it.

3. Environmentally friendly

By composing out newspaper programs you use a bit of paper every moment. Consider the environmental effects of your company and other companies no longer utilizing paper programs.

4. You can digitally save your programs

By utilizing online programs you can store previous schedules. In the event you have to appear back in a previous schedule it's neatly arranged online. In case you've got a program that's similar or equal to some previous weeks program you can replicate the program and change it slightly rather than needing to rewrite the entire program, saving you more time.

5. Alerts workers when they'll work

If your workers have alarms turned on whenever they will need to operate, they could obtain an email or text reminder they are scheduled to do the job. This reminder can aid with workers who have difficulty keeping an eye on if they're scheduled to do the job.

After reading this informative article hopefully you are able to see the advantages to moving this procedure to online instead of keep to hand write whenever your workers will do the job.

Online work at home business

Before you get caught up in the euphoria of an internet work at home company, dreaming of escaping by the overbearing boss rather than having to commute an hour each way to work, you have to ask yourself "are you really satisfied to working in your home?".

For some folks the answer is really no. They carry on a job at home company with a work mindset expecting to replace their present monthly paychecks with their brand new online work at home company all over 30 days with hardly any work or financial investment. If it seems like you; quit reading and start enjoying your work and boss longer. But if it is not, keep reading.

What is not an internet work at home company

A website. Too a lot of people that by setting up a web site, the purchasing public will soon come. No, however. A site isn't a company but an instrument to market your services or products.

A function in home job. Working for someone else where the hourly rate is ordered by a supervisor, despite the fact that you not doing so in your home, remains work. It is not a business enterprise.

Offline companies. Rupert murdoch's paper empire is a offline company to the primary part with a few internet thrown in. Mostly they market physical papers that you purchase in a store. That is the majority of their business enterprise. 1 day this could change at which the balance swings in favor of becoming an internet company, but maybe not right now.

So what's an internet work at home business

Ebay. Goods and services have been purchased on the internet. The vendor arranges her or his merchandise to ebay and as soon as they're sold, they're sent to the buyer. There perhaps some offline work involved with packaging products and submitting them but basically ebay is an internet enterprise.

Amazon. Definitely an internet work at home company with the choice of never having to package and send your merchandise to the end purchaser. Amazon as a fulfilment app where they will deliver your saved items to your clients for you personally, for a charge of course.

Network marketing. Most network marketing businesses offer you the support of delivering their merchandise right to their client's door and paying for their partners a commission for producing the sale. Clients in some instances can register online, purchase merchandise, cover the network advertising firm and also have their goods delivered to their door. A couple direct sales firms have their representatives send products to your client and collect payment. This version is growing more rare however.

An online work at home company with the ideal mindset can be going on a part-time basis and assembled to a complete time income. Being online also lets you run them from any place on earth.

3 steps to earning money on working out of home

If you're searching for an extremely straightforward but extremely powerful and also very rewarding means to begin making money online then this info will be quite helpful for you. It isn't important if you haven't ever attempted to begin your own company or whether you've tried and failed several times previously.

Learning this easy to follow step method to making money online might be exactly what you want to begin and begin seeing actual results. If for whatever reason you're skeptical about that, that is quite clear and it means that you're taking this thing seriously, that can be great:)

However let us look beyond the disbelief for a minute and think about the probable advantages you might have the ability to relish, by you picking to make this opportunity work for you.

3 earning money online working from home benefits

+ benefit - for most people having the ability to make money without having to cope with each the pressures and hassles of working for somebody else is a valuable chance. This also gives you the chance to begin your own company and be in control of your earnings.

+ longer time control - once you've learned how to utilize the world wide web to boost your income you'll have a great deal more flexibility and control on everything you could do and if it is possible to get it done. Whether spending additional time with family members and friends or studying a new hobby or skill, with your own internet based business can provide you that additional flexibility.

+ unlimited income potential - since you'll be able to market to an infinite amount of individuals in several distinct markets, there's absolutely not any limitation to the total amount of income which you may potentially earn. Your drive and ambition is going to be the largest factors in deciding your final amount of success.

All these are merely a couple of the many benefits which you could expect to appreciate as a result of spending time and effort to understand how to produce your own internet business. Now lets have a glance in the 3 key steps required.

3 steps to earning money on working out of home

Creating a huge online company that produces a huge quantity of income does call for a good deal of resources, coordination and energy. Nevertheless getting started online with a small internet based home business could be achieved using these 3 measures:

Measure 1.) Locate a profitable market - this is your main step to understand as when you do this step right you'll come to realize that the additional measures will be easier and more intriguing also. This procedure will involve a few industry research to learn what people want to know more about buying online in addition to personal reflection concerning what sort of market you'll get an interest in operating in.

Measure 2.) Construct a list - after you've got your favorite marketplace you will currently be prepared to function on collecting information from curious internet browsers inside your preferred market. This may be achieved by producing a site, supplying a totally free gift for joining the email list and utilizing an autoresponder to control the particulars of your listing and to help you develop a fantastic relationship together.

Measure 3.) Economy related products - when you've got an increasing list of people who are interested in a specific marketplace (or market) and you've begun building a fantastic relationship together, now you can begin promoting associated (money making) supplies to them.

All these are the 3 steps to earning money online working at home. The trick to success is to examine, practice and repeat this procedure over and over again till you're finding the results you would like.

Don't miss out!

Visit the website below and you can sign up to receive emails whenever Daniel D. Coffman publishes a new book. There's no charge and no obligation.

https://books2read.com/r/B-A-VRLAB-GBEOC

BOOKS 2 READ

Connecting independent readers to independent writers.

Did you love *Work Online: Become a Solopreneur, Start Working Remotely. The Complete Guide to Grow Your Company on the Internet.*? Then you should read *Freelance Consulting: Provide Services to High Ticket Customers. Build and Grow Your own Gig Empire.*[1] by Daniel D. Coffman!

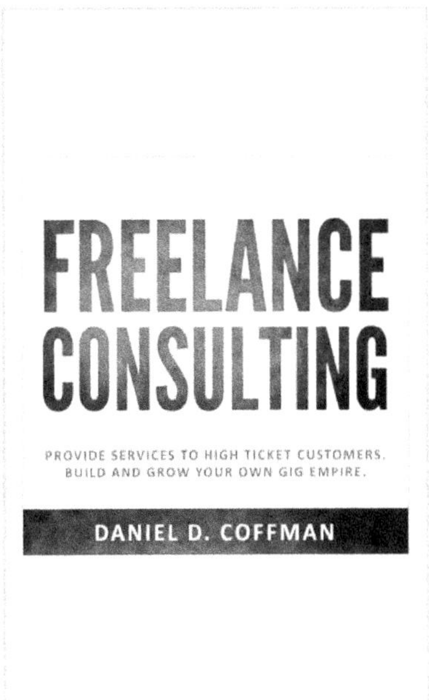

[2]

How to take the headache out of starting your own Freelance Consulting Business.

Are you tired of working for others? Have you always been dreaming of starting your own business and being your own boss? Do your friends always turn to you for advice?

If your answer to all these questions is yes, then, starting your own consulting business is something you definitely should do.

Nowadays, running a successful business has never been more complex and the need for good consultants has never been greater.

A consultant's only job is to provide good advice. Nothing more, nothing less. And, in this day and age, almost anyone can be a consultant. All you need

---

1. https://books2read.com/u/mgRyB6

2. https://books2read.com/u/mgRyB6

is to be good at helping others and find the industry you're interested in. There isn't some secret gift that will make one consultant more successful than the other. However, there is one skill that separates a good consultant from a bad consultant.

What separates a good consultant from a bad consultant is a passion and drive for excellence. Oh, and one more thing! Every good consultant must be knowledgeable about the subject they are consulting in.

Here is what you can learn from this book:

The easiest way get your freelance consulting business up and running 11 strategies for making customers come to you ***9 surefire tactics that will help you boost your business*** Top tools every freelance business must have ***The greatest mistakes consulting business owners must avoid at all cost...*** and much more!

Starting any business is a challenge, but starting a business where your goal is to help others run their own is doubly challenging. **This book will help you prepare yourself for running a business on your own and it will guide you every step of the way!**

The time has finally come for you to become independent and start your own business. The tips and tricks you find in this book will undoubtedly guide you to success!

Also by Daniel D. Coffman

Freelance Consulting: Provide Services to High Ticket Customers. Build and Grow Your own Gig Empire.
Work Online: Become a Solopreneur, Start Working Remotely. The Complete Guide to Grow Your Company on the Internet.

About the Author

Daniel D. Coffman has over 20 years of experience as a consultant with various large consulting firms and as an independent. His professional expertise spans more than 50 different industries in which he has worked as a consultant for his clients. He has seen everything from the smallest one-man operation to the largest corporation.

Creafe Publishing
CREATIVITY ¦ FUN ¦ EXPERTISE

About the Publisher

CREATIVITY ¦ FUN ¦ EXPERTISE

Our imprint Creafe Publishing, where creativity meets expertise, is your destination for a captivating array of books. Our extensive collection features a harmonious blend of non-fiction treasures and engaging fiction gems. We believe that learning should be an enjoyable adventure, and our commitment to 'Creativity ¦ Fun ¦ Expertise' is evident in every page we produce. Explore our catalog to discover knowledge and entertainment like never before. With Creafe Publishing, your reading journey is bound to be a delightful and enlightening experience.

9 798223 448198